لا إله إلا الله محمد رسول الله

Facebook Fatwa:

Saudi Clerics, Wahhabi Islam, and Social Media

Jonathan Schanzer Steven Miller

FDD PRESS

A DIVISION OF THE

FOUNDATION FOR DEFENSE OF DEMOCRACIES

WASHINGTON, D.C.

Printed in the United States of America
First Edition

ISBN: 978-0-9819712-6-1

Publication design: Basis / www.basisbranding.com

Table of Contents

Acknowledgements

This monograph is FDD's second study that draws from social media trends in the Middle East. Building upon the intense debate surrounding *P@lestinian Pulse*, FDD again partnered with the technology company ConStrat. We asked our tech partners to gather and process 6 months of social media data to better understand the online activism of religious clerics in Saudi Arabia.

Early on, we wondered whether there would be enough information to write our study. But we pushed on. After working with ConStrat to iron out those initial kinks, they once again exceeded our expectations.

We extend a special thank you to Younes Safaa, ConStrat's lead researcher for this project. His careful eye for detail, not to mention his insights into Islamic cultural and linguistic nuances, was indispensable in helping us shape this study.

We also wish to thank Abram Shanedling of The Dershowitz Group. Abram's patience, energy, and enthusiasm for this project were a model of professionalism.

Matthew Langley deserves kudos for the cover design and layout of this book. He worked within somewhat difficult legal confines, and balanced the opinions of two authors, not to mention a host of others.

During the proofreading phase, Debbie Rubin and Elana Harris Schanzer flagged many mistakes and inconsistencies, and saved us from ourselves.

Two friends of FDD, Ali Alyami and Ali Al-Ahmed, were kind enough to read our work and offer suggestions for improving it. Both men are natives of Saudi Arabia, and both share a deep interest in seeing their country implement reforms.

At FDD, our colleagues David Barnett, David Donadio, Sebastian Gorka, Laura Grossman, and Thomas Joscelyn provided valuable editorial feedback, while Reuel Marc Gerecht was admirably brutal in assessing our penultimate draft. Interns Andrew Rauth and Phil Cofone provided invaluable assistance in fact-checking.

Finally, we offer our deepest thanks to the Myron Zimmerman Philanthropic Fund and the Lisa and Michael Leffell Foundation. Without their vision and support, this project would never have seen the light of day.

—Jonathan Schanzer and Steven Miller

Acknowledgement

Glossary

ahadith (sing. *hadith*)	sayings of the Prophet Muhammad
da'wa	Islamic call/outreach
deen	religion
fatwa (pl. *fatawa*)	religious opinion
fiqh	Islamic jurisprudence
fitna	discord
haram	forbidden
ifta	issuing a *fatwa* or *fatawa*
ikhwan	brothers; refers to the Arabian nomads converted into a religiously zealous fighting force by Wahhabi leaders during the early 20th century. Also a term used to described the Muslim Brotherhood (al-Ikhwan al-Muslimun)
imam	prayer leader; leader of Muslim community
jahiliya	age of religious ignorance; commonly used to refer to the Arabs' religious ignorance in pre-Islamic Arabia
jihad	struggle; fighting in the name of God
jizyah	tax historically levied against non-Muslims in Muslim nations
khaleefa (also, *khalifa*)	caliph; leader of the unified Muslim community (*ummah*), which is governed by the Islamic legal code (*Shari'ah*)
kuffar (sing. *kafir*)	infidels; those who are blasphemous
madrasa (pl. *madaaris*)	school; often used to refer to schools of Islamic education

Maktab al-Khidamat	Services Office; founded in Peshawar, Pakistan by Osama bin Laden in 1984 to recruit and train fighters opposed to the Soviet presence in Afghanistan; precursor to the al-Qaeda network. Also known as MAK
mujahideen (sing. *mujahid*)	Islamic fighters
niqab	full body veil
Quran	Islam's central holy text, considered to be the word of God
sahwa	awakening
al-Salaf al-Salih	righteous ancestors; refers to the first three Muslim generations as embodied by: the Prophet Muhammad's Companions (*sahaba*); the Companions' followers (*tabi'in*); and the followers' followers (*tabi'i al-tabi'in*)
salafi	those who follow the religious example of *al-salaf al-salih*, Islam's righteous ancestors
Shari'ah	Islamic legal code
sheikh	religious scholar; tribal leader
shirk	polytheism
sunnah	traditional social and legal customs of Prophet Muhammad, as preserved in eyewitness accounts from his disciples of his words, actions and approbations
tafseer (also, *tafsir*)	Quranic commentary by religious scholars
takfeer (also, *takfir*)	labeling other Muslims as unbelievers, thereby excommunicating them from Islam
tawheed (also, *tawhid*)	doctrine of the oneness of God; monotheism; unification
ulema (sing. *alim*)	religious scholars
ummah	worldwide Muslim community

Executive Summary

Since the September 11 attacks of 2001, Saudi Arabia has undertaken efforts to curb state-sanctioned Islamic radicalism and xenophobia. However, some elements of the sanctioned establishment, coupled with a number of unsanctioned clerics, continue to produce rulings and opinions that run counter to U.S. interests. The good news is that this problem has been reduced somewhat. The bad news is that the problem still exists. More worrisome is the fact that many clerics with radical views are flocking to social media and have ever-growing numbers of followers.

Ahead of the ten-year anniversary of the 9/11 attacks, the Foundation for Defense of Democracies (FDD) commissioned a study to determine the extent to which the Saudi clergy maintains a presence on the Internet, and how they and their followers promote Wahhabi ideology online. FDD selected ConStrat, a Washington, D.C.-based technology company, to collect and analyze the data for this study.[1] ConStrat used proprietary software usually deployed on behalf of the U.S. government.

Over the course of six months (January 1 through June 30, 2011), ConStrat's researchers collected and coded data from more than 40,000 entries on Arabic and English language websites, forum threads, and social media posts by Saudi clerics or social media commentary about the clerics. Those entries are the basis of this study.

It is important to note that, even with the wide reach of ConStrat's proprietary software, this study could not possibly cover the entire social media environment in question. Moreover, the data derived from this study provided only one stream of intelligence about Saudi society, and does not paint the full picture of how the Saudi religious establishment propagates its ideology. However, as was the case with our last study that deployed ConStrat's technology,[2] we undertook this project with the assumption that online discourse can provide unique insights into a specific area of inquiry.

The tone and tenor of the conversations ConStrat coded was mixed, but was generally marked by an absence of overt militancy. This does not, however,

1 For more information about ConStrat, please visit www.constrat.net.

2 Jonathan Schanzer & Mark Dubowitz, *P@lestinian Pulse: What Policymakers Can Learn From Palestinian Social Media*, (Washington, DC: FDD Press, 2010).

indicate an absence of intolerant or xenophobic positions. According to the data scored with ConStrat's proprietary VX software, views that were hostile to America, the West, and non-Muslim or secular cultures represented nearly 52 percent of the English data, while in Arabic they represented 75 percent.

In addition to social media outlets like Twitter, Facebook, and YouTube, other technology such as Apple iPhone, iPad, and iPod touch applications are popular among the Saudi clerics. This phenomenon contradicts the religious establishment's historical opposition to "corrupting" modern technology. Indeed, the clerics understand that these are powerful tools through which they can spread their messages.

Saudi Arabia's success in reducing militant online content is a positive sign that the Saudi government can, when sufficiently motivated, temper the radicalism that percolates in the kingdom. This is also a sign that when the U.S. properly applies pressure, it can have a noticeable impact.

However, the kingdom's recent attempts to convince the West that it is promoting "religious tolerance" and embracing change do not resonate with the content mined during this study. Saudi Arabia's religious establishment—both sanctioned and unsanctioned—still openly denigrates other religions and cultures, and fails in many ways to adapt to modern social and scientific concepts. That is troubling, given that Saudi Arabia is often described as one of the United States' most important Middle East allies. Indeed, this stark lack of shared values has encumbered the relationship in the past, and does not bode well for the future.

With new media tools in their hands, Saudi clerics are now communicating with the Saudi public and wider Muslim world on an unprecedented scale. To be sure, the relatively free flow of information in Saudi Arabia should be welcomed. But there may be a downside; as the unsanctioned clerics increasingly turn to various social media platforms, the Saudi regime may find controlling their messages more difficult. In this way, emboldened clerics may eventually pose a direct challenge to the regime. Indeed, social media contributed to the upheaval that rocked the Middle East in 2011, and American policymakers should be aware of this possibility.

The Saudi social media environment is further deserving of ongoing observation by the intelligence community (for threats) and State Department (for diplomacy and de-radicalization). We have long held that, coupled with other reporting streams, online research can greatly enhance our understanding of complex policy problems. In Saudi Arabia's case, where access to the country is extremely limited and its press is severely restricted, thorough online research can be of value.

MAP OF SAUDI ARABIA

Introduction

As the custodian of Islam's two holy cities, Mecca and Medina, the Kingdom of Saudi Arabia has undeniable influence in the Muslim world. During the Eisenhower Administration, officials began referring to the Saudi monarch as the "Islamic pope."[1] As Saudi scholar Madawi al-Rasheed notes, "The symbolic significance of Saudi Arabia for Islam and Muslims cannot be overestimated."[2]

While the royal al-Saud lineage is viewed as the rightful heir to the kingdom, it lacks religious credentials. To compensate, the monarchy relies on the descendants of Muhammad ibn Abdul Wahhab, the Al al-Sheikh lineage, who preach the ascetic Salafi version of Islam indigenous to Saudi Arabia, now known as Wahhabism. Thus, the Al al-Sheikh and other prominent religious families provide the House of Saud with religious authority, which bolsters its credibility at home and defends it from religious detractors abroad.

The Clerical Class

The official religious establishment in Saudi Arabia is structured around several key institutions, chief among them the Council of Senior Ulema (CSU)[3] and the Permanent Committee for Research and Ifta (issuing religious decrees).[4] These religious authorities offer state-sanctioned *fatawa* (religious decrees) on major social and political issues in the kingdom, and offer advice directly to the Saudi king.

While it is difficult to pinpoint exact numbers of Saudi clergy, according to research conducted by the U.S. Army between 1986 and 1998, "the *Ulema* (religious scholars) and their families included an estimated 7,000 to 10,000

1 Rachel Bronson, *Thicker Than Oil: America's Uneasy Partnership with Saudi Arabia*, (NY: Oxford University Press, 2006), p. 74.

2 Madawi al-Rasheed, *A History of Saudi Arabia (2nd edition)*, (NY: Cambridge University Press, 2010), p. 5.

3 Ondrej Beranek, "The Sword and the Book: Implications of the Intertwining of the Saudi Ruling Family and the Religious Establishment," Brandeis University Crown Center, *Middle East Brief*, No. 28, April 2008, p. 3, www.brandeis.edu/crown/publications/meb/MEB28.pdf.

4 Shmuel Bachar, Shmuel Bar, Rachel Machtiger & Yair Minzili, "Establishment Ulama and Radicalism in Egypt, Saudi Arabia, and Jordan," (Washington, DC: Hudson Institute, 2006), p. 18, www.currenttrends.org/docLib/20061226_UlamaandRadicalismfinal.pdf.

persons. However, only thirty to forty most senior scholars among them exercised substantive political influence. These prominent clergy constituted the members of the Council of Senior Ulema."[5]

The religious establishment primarily maintains influence in the judiciary and in the field of education,[6] but it also holds sway in the areas of communication and national administration.[7] Over the years, state-sanctioned clerics have directly affected U.S. interests. As analyst Nawaf Obaid notes, the *Ulema* provided religious cover for the Saudi government when it imposed an oil embargo following the 1973 Yom Kippur War, allowed U.S. troops onto Saudi soil in 1990, permitted those forces to remain after the war, and supported the Taliban.[8] These are just a few examples. One could also argue that the clerics' contribution to the overall Wahhabi proselytizing effort, which resulted in the radicalization of untold numbers of Muslim youth worldwide, has had a larger impact than all of those events combined.

But the clerics' influence should not be overstated. The clerics often act as a rubber stamp for Saudi state policies. Indeed, they often issue decrees only after the ruling family makes a policy decision. Furthermore, they largely refrain from wading into politics, and occasionally issue *fatawa* solely to remind citizens of their obligatory submission to Saudi political will.

The government's control of all clerical appointments confirms this dynamic.[9] In early 2009, King Abdullah demonstrated as much when he ordered a major reshuffling of the Saudi government, including several high-level religious positions. One official removed was Saleh al-Luhaidan, the chief judge of the Supreme Judiciary Council and member of the Council of Senior Ulema. Al-Luhaidan attracted unwanted attention in September 2008 when he declared it permissible to kill the owners of satellite television channels that promote moral depravity.[10]

The Unsanctioned Clerics

However, these clerics and the CSU do not represent the entire Saudi religious establishment. Many other clerics—the unsanctioned ones—do not serve

5 Helen Chapin Metz, ed., "Saudi Arabia: A Country Study," (Washington, DC: GPO for the Library of Congress, 1992), http://countrystudies.us/saudi-arabia/54.htm.

6 "The Role of the Ulema (Religious Leaders)," *Saudi Arabia Market Information Resource (SAMIRAD)*, www.saudinf.com/main/c3.htm.

7 David Commins, *The Wahhabi Mission and Saudi Arabia*, (London: I.B. Tauris, 2009), p. 105.

8 Nawaf E. Obaid, "The Power of Saudi Arabia's Islamic Leaders," *Middle East Quarterly*, September 1999, pp. 51-58, www.meforum.org/482/the-power-of-saudi-arabias-islamic-leaders.

9 "Can Saudi Arabia Reform Itself?" International Crisis Group, *Middle East Report*, July 14, 2004, p. 6. www.crisisgroup.org/~/media/Files/Middle East North Africa/Iran Gulf/Saudi Arabia/Can Saudi Arabia Reform Itself.ashx.

10 "Major Reshuffle in Saudi Arabia," BBC News, February 14, 2009, http://news.bbc.co.uk/2/hi/middle_east/7890211.stm.

directly as the state's religious agents. Though they hold positions at a number of the kingdom's universities and preach at mosques throughout the country, the government solicits neither their advice nor their *fatawa*.

Because they face fewer constraints from the regime, the unsanctioned clerics can offer deeper insights into Wahhabism, including its jihadi strain and its xenophobic views of non-Muslims and the West. At other times, as was the case in the late 1970s and early 1990s, they can even pose a direct challenge to the regime.[11]

Arguably, the most famous group of unsanctioned clerics in Saudi Arabia were the *Sahwa* (Awakening) clerics, who traced their roots back to the 1960s and the flight of the Muslim Brotherhood to the kingdom from Egypt, Iraq, and Syria, which were then pan-Arabist, secular regimes hostile to Islamist groups.[12] The *Sahwa* clerics synthesized traditional Salafi-Wahhabi theological teachings with the Brothers' belief that intertwining society and politics is a religious imperative. Inspired by the Brotherhood's political activism, the popular *Sahwa* reinterpreted the Saudi creed.[13]

In 1990, as Saddam Hussein's army advanced into Kuwait, the *Sahwa* made headlines for their ardent opposition to King Fahd's reliance on the U.S.-led military coalition to defend the Arabian Peninsula. The palace's decision to allow non-Muslim forces into the kingdom, legitimized with a *fatwa* by Grand Mufti Abdulaziz ibn Baz, stoked the ire of Salman al-Odah and Safar al-Hawali, two well-known clerical firebrands from the *Sahwa*. Between 1991 and 1992, the *Sahwa* called for greater Islamization of Saudi society, criticized the submissive state clerics, and demanded that unsanctioned clerics have more say in social and foreign affairs.[14] The *Sahwa* issued a direct challenge to the Saudis state, via two widely circulated letters, calling for reforms.

The first was the "Letter of Demands," signed by 400 scholars, which called for cleansing the state of corruption, avoiding alliances that violated Islamic law, and improving the state's religious institutions. The second, titled "Memorandum of Advice," bluntly called for the king to outlaw the teaching of Western law, to create a half-million man army to fight Israel, and to end foreign aid to atheist regimes.[15]

11 See: Mahmoun Fandy, *Saudi Arabia and the Politics of Dissent*, (NY: Palgrave, 1999).

12 Stéphane Lacroix, "Saudi Islamists and The Potential for Protest," *Foreign Policy*, June 2, 2011, http://mideast.foreignpolicy.com/posts/2011/06/02/saudi_islamists_and_the_potential_for_protest.

13 Ondrej Beranek, "Divided We Survive: A Landscape of Fragmentation in Saudi Arabia," Brandeis University Crown Center, *Middle East Brief*, No. 33, January 2009, p. 3, www.brandeis.edu/crown/publications/meb/MEB33.pdf.

14 Rachel Bronson, "Rethinking Religion: The Legacy of the U.S.-Saudi Relationship," *Washington Quarterly*, Autumn 2005, p. 127, www.twq.com/05autumn/docs/05autumn_bronson.pdf.

15 For a detailed description, see: Bronson, *Thicker Than Oil*, pp. 212-3.

The government did not tolerate this dissent. In 1994, the regime arrested al-Odah, al-Hawali, and nearly 1,300 *Sahwa* affiliates.[16] In the eyes of their followers, the resulting five-year prison term cemented the clerics' standing as courageous men. However, upon being released in 1999, under pressure from the Saudi state, the *Sahwa* splintered. Some of its members joined other Saudi Islamist movements, including jihadi groups. The state successfully silenced and co-opted others.

Today, the line separating the sanctioned religious establishment from the co-opted unsanctioned one is blurred, as many clerics now commonly defend the regime.[17] At the same time, some clerics continue to call for reforms. Al-Odah is now a quasi-government supporter, yet he backed petitions in 2011 that called for Saudi Shura (Consultation) Council elections, an end to corruption, and a constitutional monarchy.[18]

New Messages, New Media

While clerics in the 1990s issued *fatawa* and *tafseer* (Quranic commentary by religious scholars) via audiotape, they now take their messages online. What the Saudi clerics allow us to view online, in both Arabic and English, offers a glimpse into the world of Wahhabism and the closed Saudi society.

This offers more than opportunities for sociological observation; there is also an important national security component. After the 9/11 terrorist attacks, the Saudi regime came under fire for funding Wahhabi vitriol and for sponsoring terrorism through state-funded charities and banks. But it was only after a terrorist campaign inside the kingdom in 2003 and 2004, fueled by the same ideology that the country long exported, that the monarchy took steps to censor its religious network. In fact, the government began to monitor tens of thousands of mosques and schools, and employed its clerics to help "de-radicalize" extremists. Eliminating radical online content was also a major focus of this effort.

The Saudi monarchy undoubtedly took some positive steps, but Wahhabi ideology is still spreading. Ahead of the 10-year anniversary of the 9/11 attacks,

16 Bachar, Bar, Machtiger & Minzili, *Establishment Ulama and Radicalism in Egypt, Saudi Arabia, and Jordan*, p. 18.

17 When al-Qaeda in the Arabian Peninsula (AQAP) attacked three foreign housing complexes in Riyadh in May 2003, killing 34 and injuring 200, clerics roundly condemned the attacks and the perpetrators. See Beranek, "The Sword and the Book." In December 2004, 35 sheikhs denounced London-based Saudi dissident Saad al-Faqih's attempts to foment unrest against the regime. See Toby Craig Jones, "The Clerics, the Sahwa and the Saudi State," *Center for Contemporary Conflict: Strategic Insights*, March 2005, p. 4, www.nps.edu/Academics/centers/ccc/publications/OnlineJournal/2005/Mar/jonesMar05.pdf.

18 "Municipal Elections in Saudi Arabia Next Month," *Al Jazeera*, March 23, 2011, www.aljazeera.com/news/middleeast/2011/03/2011323101416723875.html.

the Foundation for Defense of Democracies (FDD) commissioned a study to gauge the way the Wahhabi religious establishment, including both sanctioned and unsanctioned clerics, approaches topics online, from international politics to Islam. FDD selected ConStrat, a Washington, DC-based technology company, to collect and analyze the data for this study.[19] ConStrat used proprietary software usually deployed on behalf of the U.S. government.

With protests raging across the Middle East since December 2010, secular and Islamist reformers have harnessed social media to hasten the downfall of autocrats. It should then come as no surprise that Saudi clerics conduct much of their outreach through social media, too.

Over the course of six months (January 1 through June 30, 2011), ConStrat collected and coded data from more than 40,000 entries on Arabic and English websites, forum threads, social media posts by Saudi clerics, and social media commentary about the clerics. These entries form the basis of our study, which took place during a fascinating time in Saudi Arabia and the Middle East.

It is important to note here that FDD's research was limited to the analysis of 40,000 entries. Even with the wide reach of ConStrat's proprietary software, we could not possibly cover the entire social media environment related to the Saudi clerics. But, as was the case with *P@lestinian Pulse*, the last study in which we applied ConStrat's technology,[20] we undertook this project assuming that a representative sample can provide unique insights into Saudi religious and societal trends.

Based on our findings, we believe the Saudi religious establishment is less overtly radical than in the past. However, radical ideas and strong xenophobic currents still exist. In many ways, the clerical establishment provides religious cover for the Saudi government when it adopts positions that run counter to our interests and values.

Facebook Fatwa provides a glimpse of the Saudi religious establishment's online activities during a critical moment for the Middle East, U.S.-Saudi relations, and the kingdom itself, where Wahhabism continues to reverberate thanks to a potent combination of old traditions and new technology.

19 For more information about ConStrat, please visit www.constrat.net.

20 Schanzer & Dubowitz, *P@lestinian Pulse*.

The Evolution of Wahhabism: From Takfeer to Twitter

In 1740, Muhammad ibn Abdul Wahhab began his mission to eradicate religious innovations in Basra, part of present-day Iraq, initiating the Islamic revivalist movement now known as Wahhabism.[1]

Wahhabism is an expression of the ascetic Salafi Islam, a branch of Sunni Islam that seeks to revive "true" monotheism, as embodied by the Prophet Muhammad and his followers (*al-Salaf al-Salih*). Wahhabism rests on the belief that all laws for men are proscribed in the *Quran*–Islam's central holy text, considered the word of God–leaving virtually no room for interpretation. Abdul Wahhab insisted that religious scholars (*ulema*) strictly follow only the *Quran* and *Sunnah* (traditional social and legal customs of Prophet Muhammad) for guidance.[2] By relying solely on the *Quran* and *Sunnah*, Wahhabism challenges and disregards centuries of Islamic jurisprudence (*fiqh*), theology, and traditions.[3]

As a result of his strict interpretation of the religion, Abdul Wahhab gained few friends during the early years. He left Basra shortly after he began preaching, and went to al-Uyayna in northeastern Arabia. But the leader of al-Uyayna soon forced Abdul Wahhab to leave the town, after he personally destroyed the tomb built on the grave of Zayd ibn al-Khattab—brother of the second Muslim caliph Umar—and burned two famous religious works for their "idolatrous" expressions.[4] Ironically, in at least three Saudi towns, Abdul Wahhab himself was denounced as a misguided religious innovator for these desecrations.[5]

But in 1744, he found political protection for his mission when he met Muhammad ibn Saud, the leader of the central Arabian oasis settlement of al-Dir'iyya. Abdul Wahhab explained his view that the people of central Arabia

1 Commins, *The Wahhabi Mission and Saudi Arabia*, p. 17.

2 "Sunnah," *Encyclopedia Britannica* (Online), 2011, www.britannica.com/EBchecked/topic/573993/Sunnah.

3 Ahmad Moussalli, "Wahhabism, Salafism, and Islamism: Who is the Enemy?" *Conflicts Forum*, January 2009, pp. 4-6, www.conflictsforum.org/briefings/Wahhabism-Salafism-and-Islamism.pdf.

4 Sheikh Jamaal al Din Zarabozo, *The Life, Teachings and Influence of Muhammad ibn Abdul-Wahhab*, (Saudi Arabia: Ministry of Islamic Affairs, Endowments, Dawah, and Guidance, 2005), p. 30, www.sultan.org/books/wahhabism.pdf.

5 Commins, *The Wahhabi Mission and Saudi Arabia*, p. 20.

(Najd) were living in religious ignorance (*jahiliya*) and should return to a purer version of Islam. The men pledged their mutual support for each other, thus sealing the enduring Saudi-Wahhabi pact.[6]

The Saudi-Wahhabi mission aggressively expanded, and became the dominant religious doctrine in Arabia by the end of the 18th century.[7] The Wahhabis conquered al-Qatif and al-Ahsa in eastern Arabia, extended southeast to the modern-day United Arab Emirates, south to the ports of Yemen (which they failed to hold), and northward into Iraq and the Syrian Desert.[8] But Saudi-Wahhabi expansion soon threatened the Ottoman Empire when it reached the Hijaz in western Arabia, bringing the Ottomans and Saudis closer to conflict.

The Wahhabis continued to march even after Abdul Wahhab's death in 1792.[9] The mission took control over Islam's two holiest cities, Mecca and Medina, between 1803 and 1805.[10] With the support of Abdul Wahhab's followers, Abdullah ibn Saud became the new Saudi leader. However, the powerful Ottoman-Egyptian army soon thrust into the Saudi-Wahhabi heartland, and captured Abdullah. In 1818, the Ottomans guaranteed him safe passage to Constantinople, only to behead and impale him.[11]

The Wahhabi establishment suffered great losses, including the death of some two dozen *Ulema* and men of scholarly lineages. Remarkably, this did not destroy the Wahhabis or their ideology. Descendants of Abdul Wahhab and Abdullah's son, Turki, revived the mission just six years later,[12] but they lacked the expansionary zeal of Abdullah's rule.

This second emirate was short-lived. It crumbled in 1884 amid fratricidal strife within the Saudi family.[13] Nevertheless, this brief period of transition (1824-1884) was critical to the Wahhabis' self-preservation. They soon reunited with the Saudi family, and forged the most important oil-producing state of the 20th century.[14]

The Modern State

With a mix of might and religion similar to that of the initial Saudi-Wahhabi conquest, the al-Saud and Wahhabi loyalists set about reclaiming Arabia from Ottoman rule under the leadership of Abdulaziz ibn Saud. With Al al-Sheikh

6 Ibid., p. 19.

7 Al-Rasheed, *A History of Saudi Arabia*, pp. 17-22.

8 Nadav Safran, *Saudi Arabia: The Ceaseless Quest for Security,* (NY: Cornell University Press, 1988), p. 11.

9 Zarabozo, *The Life, Teachings and Influence of Muhammad ibn Abdul-Wahhab,* p. 54.

10 Commins, *The Wahhabi Mission and Saudi Arabia,* pp. 30-31.

11 Safran, *Saudi Arabia: The Ceaseless Quest for Security,* pp. 13-14.

12 Commins, *The Wahhabi Mission and Saudi Arabia,* pp. 43-44.

13 Safran, *Saudi Arabia: The Ceaseless Quest for Security,* pp. 16-19.

14 Commins, *The Wahhabi Mission and Saudi Arabia,* p. 66.

and British assistance, ibn Saud brought the region under Wahhabi control by December 1925, and declared the modern Kingdom of Saudi Arabia in 1932.[15]

The success of this re-conquest was due, in part, to a group of religious zealots known as the *Ikhwan* (Brothers). The *Ikhwan* were nomads from the tribal confederations of Arabia who converted to Wahhabism, and served as a military force for ibn Saud. By 1914, they developed a reputation as uncompromising religious soldiers who enforced monotheism, and harshly punished those who refused to follow the "true path."[16]

As the *Ikhwan* conquered towns and ruthlessly killed nomads who refused to convert—including women and children—ibn Saud earned enemies. Between 1914 and 1926, ibn Saud and Wahhabi leaders tried to moderate the *Ikhwan's* behavior. In January and February 1927, ibn Saud and Wahhabi *ulema* met with *Ikhwan* leaders at a conference in Riyadh. The *Ikhwan* demanded strict laws to govern the Shi'a, the minority sect traditionally maligned in Wahhabi Islam. Ibn Saud accepted their demands, but demanded that they recognize him as the only legitimate authority on matters of foreign policy and *jihad*. He further banned them from conducting raids on British territory in Iraq and Transjordan.[17]

Despite this agreement, the *Ikhwan* remained disgruntled about having to temper their role as raiders and religious enforcers, which afforded them wealth and opportunities to lord over newly conquered towns in Arabia.[18]

Finally, in December 1928, the confrontation came to a head, as the Ikhwan raided a caravan of merchants in the Wahhabi stronghold of Burayda, which ibn Saud perceived as an attack on his people. He responded by sending his troops to put down the Ikhwan. The two sides battled from March 1929 to January 1930, when the *Ikhwan* eventually surrendered.

Rather than simply punishing the *Ikhwan*, ibn Saud relied on a mix of punishment and religious rehabilitation.[19] This was not the last time that the Saudi state's zealous religious indoctrination ultimately wreaked havoc on internal stability. Nor would it be the last time the Saudi state applied a questionable cocktail of punishment and rehabilitation to regain control.

15 Al-Rasheed, *A History of Saudi Arabia*, pp. 44-46.

16 Ibid., pp. 56-59.

17 Commins, *The Wahhabi Mission and Saudi Arabia,* pp. 88-89.

18 Ibid.

19 Ibid., pp. 90-91.

Oil and the Cold War

During the 20th century, notes Jim Woolsey, former CIA director and chairman of the Foundation for Defense of Democracies, the relationship between the United States and Saudi Arabia "was a reasonably close and relaxed one." This was primarily due to the fact that "we were on the same side in the Cold War, and the Saudis valued our support (and we theirs) against Soviet influence in the Middle East."[20]

But the cornerstone of the relationship has always been oil. King ibn Saud awarded the first oil concession to Standard Oil of California (SOCAL) in 1933, which the company in turn granted to its subsidiary, the California Arabian Standard Oil Company (CASOC). Five years later, CASOC struck oil at the Dammam-7 well, cementing the U.S.-Saudi relationship with a simple formula: Saudi oil powered the American economy and simultaneously enriched the monarchy.[21]

The value of this relationship increased for both sides during World War II, when the United States military needed more oil and the Saudis needed to protect their oil fields from the Axis powers. Italian warplanes attempted to bomb oil fields in Bahrain and eastern Saudi Arabia in November 1940, and though the Italians missed their targets, many of CASOC's employees fled back to the U.S. In 1941, when the Germans threatened to invade Dhahran, the rest of CASOC's camp there evacuated.[22]

In 1943, President Roosevelt made Saudi Arabia eligible for the Lend-Lease program, designed to offer U.S. allies assistance and bolster American security around the world. Saudi Arabia qualified because of its importance to the global oil market, its strategic location in the Persian Gulf, and King ibn Saud's influence in the Arab and Muslim worlds.[23] In 1944, the Arabian American Oil Company (ARAMCO), an outgrowth of CASOC, began developing the kingdom's infrastructure beyond the oil fields. This included roads, railways, pipelines, ports, and airports to facilitate the oil business, but also included schools and hospitals.[24]

But the Saudi government felt short-changed when in 1949 it received just $39.1 million in royalties and fees from ARAMCO, while the U.S. Treasury received $43 million in U.S. income tax revenues. However, the Saudis

20 R. James Woolsey, "Foreword," in *Saudi Publications on Hate Ideology Fill American Mosques*, (Washington, DC: Freedom House, 2005), p. 7.

21 Bronson, *Thicker Than Oil*, pp. 17-21.

22 Ibid., p. 20.

23 Ibid., p. 40. According to Bronson, the U.S. provided the Saudis with $99 million in aid between 1940 and 1947, just 25 percent of which was to be repaid.

24 Al-Rasheed, *A History of Saudi Arabia*, p. 92.

got over their grievances, as the State Department advanced the "50/50" agreement, which divided oil revenues evenly between ARAMCO and the Saudi government, and granted the Saudis important tax advantages. By 1951, ARAMCO paid U.S. income taxes of just $6 million, while it paid the Saudi government almost $110 million.[25]

Throughout the 20th century, the U.S.-Saudi relationship remained mostly stable. Of course, the Arab-Israeli conflict was a challenge. The most significant breach of the U.S.-Saudi relationship came in October 1973, when President Nixon helped Israel battle back against a surprise attack from the Syrians and Egyptians. As the war ensued, and the U.S. helped Israel regain its footing, Saudi Arabia and other Arab oil-producers imposed an embargo that sent oil prices rising 70 percent.[26]

While painful, the embargo lasted less than six months. Since then, notwithstanding occasional crises, the Saudi government has had a strong interest in keeping oil flowing and maintaining smooth relations with the U.S. As global demand for oil increased, the wealth of the royal family grew.

Rolling Back Communism

Rolling back Communism was another key aspect of the U.S.-Saudi relationship after World War II. To the Saudis, the Communists were godless expansionists who allied with secular pan-Arabist regimes. Similarly, the Communists not only threatened America's allies across Europe and Asia, but also the country's core values, including political freedoms, free enterprise, and freedom of religion.

In the 1970s, oil wealth enabled the Saudis to fight Communism with more than $7.5 billion in foreign and military aid to countries like Egypt, Syria, Pakistan, North Yemen, Sudan, and others. Saudi funding was particularly instrumental in supporting anti-Soviet (and anti-Libyan) operations and alliances in Angola, Chad, Eritrea, and Somalia. The Saudis' financial role in combating Communism became increasingly vital, especially as the United States struggled with the fallout from Vietnam, Watergate, and domestic intelligence scandals.[27]

Though successful, financing covert operations and forming anti-Soviet coalitions were not the Saudis' only strategies. They also employed religion.

Exporting Radicalism

In 1962, ibn Saud's son, Faisal, who became king in 1964, founded the Muslim

25 Bronson, *Thicker Than Oil*, pp. 55-56.

26 Al-Rasheed, *A History of Saudi Arabia*, pp. 131-134.

27 Bronson, *Thicker Than Oil*, pp. 129-130.

World League (MWL) to facilitate the global propagation of Wahhabism. Faisal intended the MWL to challenge Shi'a, Sufis, and other "heretical" Muslim sects. To further that objective in South Asia, the MWL backed the Deobandis[28] and other Salafi fundamentalist groups ideologically akin to Wahhabis. Meanwhile, the Saudis sent missionaries and funding for Islamic schools to countries in West Africa, including Nigeria, Mali, Ghana, Ivory Coast, and Guinea.[29]

As the first major Islamic organization created by the Saudis, the MWL proved integral to spreading the Wahhabi mission. As chairman of the MWL's Constituent Council during the Afghan *jihad* of the 1980s, Saudi Grand Mufti Abdulaziz ibn Baz emphasized the responsibility of Islamic states and organizations to support *mujahideen* (Islamic fighters) wherever they fought.[30]

Several Saudi-based subsidiaries of the MWL soon emerged around the world, including the World Assembly of Muslim Youth (WAMY) in 1972, the International Islamic Relief Organization (IIRO) in 1979,[31] and al-Haramain Foundation in the early 1990s.[32] WAMY's goal was to spread monotheism (*tawheed*) and to arm "the Muslim youth with full confidence in the supremacy of the Islamic system over other systems."[33] WAMY distributed works from prominent Muslim Brotherhood ideologue Sayyid Qutb, as well as Mawlana Abu al-Ala Mawdudi, the leader of the radical Pakistani political party Jamaat-i-Islami.[34] As recently as 2003, WAMY and the IIRO still funded the Palestinian terrorist organization Hamas.[35]

28 The website of the Deobandi religious institution Darul-Uloom, founded in Deoband, India, cites a passage from the book *Modern Islam in India*, by Professor W. Cantwell Smith of McGill University: "Deoband is thoroughly dissatisfied with things as they are, and it is vigorous and determined in its efforts to improve them. Its aim is to resuscitate classical Islam, rid the Muslims of the theological corruption[s], the ritual degradation[s] and the material exploitation[s] to which they have fallen prey since the British occupation... Deoband 'Ulama' are puritanically strict. They work assiduously to overcome and destroy backsliding, superstitions, saint-worship and all the paraphernalia of ignorance, poverty and fear in a depressed and decadent agrarian society." See the Darul-Uloom website www.darululoom-deoband.com/english/index.htm.

29 Commins, *The Wahhabi Mission and Saudi Arabia*, pp. 152-3.

30 Dore Gold, *Hatred's Kingdom: How Saudi Arabia Supports the New Global Terrorism*, (Washington, DC: Regnery Publishing, 2004), p. 119.

31 For the International Islamic Relief Organization's website, see www.egatha.org/portal/index.php?option=com_content&view=frontpage&Itemid=21.

32 National Commission on Terrorist Attacks Upon the United States, *The 9/11 Commission Report*, July 22, 2004, pp. 170 & 372, www.911commission.gov/report/911Report.pdf.

33 Lorenzo Vidino, "The Muslim Brotherhood's Conquest of Europe," *Middle East Quarterly*, Winter 2005, pp. 25-34, www.meforum.org/687/the-muslim-brotherhoods-conquest-of-europe.

34 Sayyid Qutb, *Milestones*, (Lahore: Kazi Publications, 2007).

35 Gold, *Hatred's Kingdom*, p. 226.

From 1973 to 2002, the Saudi government spent more than $80 billion on Islamic institutions and activities in the non-Muslim world alone, fueling the construction of more than 1,500 mosques, 150 Islamic centers, 202 Muslim colleges, and 2,000 Islamic schools.[36] As of 2002, Saudi funding produced an estimated 10,000 Deobandi-run schools in India, Pakistan, and Bangladesh. Other targets for Wahhabi outreach were countries with large Muslim populations like Albania, Kosovo, and Bosnia, where the Saudis have spent more than $600 million alone. As a result of this outreach, nearly 80 percent of all Islamic institutions in the U.S. and Canada are Saudi-sponsored, not to mention mosques and Islamic centers across Western Europe.[37]

Late 1979 marked a turning point in the evolution of modern Wahhabism. King Khaled faced an internal challenge when the Salafi separatist group *al-Jama'a al-Salafiyya al-Muhtasiba* (JSM) and its leader Juhayman al-Otaibi seized the Grand Mosque in Mecca on November 20. Ultimately, with backing from the *Ulema*, Saudi forces moved in to end the two-week stand-off.[38] Al-Otaibi and 62 other JSM members were captured and publicly beheaded.[39]

In addition to the Grand Mosque takeover, the country's estimated 15 percent Shi'a population drew inspiration from the Islamic Revolution in Iran, and staged protests in the kingdom's oil-rich Eastern Province,[40] where Shi'a represent nearly 75 percent of the population.[41] Compounding the Saudi monarch's anxiety, the Soviet Union invaded Afghanistan in December 1979, sparking fears that the country would become a launching point for Soviet expansion into southwestern Asia and the Persian Gulf oil fields.

In the eyes of King Khaled, the combination of these events threatened to undermine Saudi Arabia's leadership of Sunni Muslims, so he undertook drastic

36 Alexander Alexiev, "The Wages of Extremism: Radical Islam's Threat to the West and the Muslim World," Hudson Institute, March 2011, p. 44, www.hudson.org/files/publications/AAlexievWagesofExtremism032011.pdf.

37 Alexander Alexiev, "The End of an Alliance," *National Review*, October 28, 2002, http://old.nationalreview.com/flashback/flashback-alexiev112602.asp.

38 See: Yaroslav Trofimov, *The Siege of Mecca: The 1979 Uprising at Islam's Holiest Shrine*, (NY: Anchor Books, 2007).

39 "Mosque Has Violent Past," *The New York Times*, August 2, 1987, www.nytimes.com/1987/08/02/world/mosque-has-violent-past.html?src=pm.

40 "The Shiite Question in Saudi Arabia," The International Crisis Group, *Middle East Report*, No. 45, September 19, 2005, p. 1, www.crisisgroup.org/~/media/Files/Middle%20East%20North%20Africa/Iran%20Gulf/Saudi%20Arabia/The%20Shiite%20Question%20in%20Saudi%20Arabia.pdf; Also see: Toby Craig Jones, "Rebellion on the Saudi Periphery: Modernity, Marginalization, and the Shia Uprising of 1979," *International Journal of Middle East Studies*, Vol. 38, Issue 2, May 2006, pp. 213-233.

41 Mai Yamani, "Saudi Arabia's Shia Stand Up," *Project Syndicate*, March 11, 2009, www.project-syndicate.org/commentary/yamani20/English.

measures to reaffirm his religious credentials to Islamists at home and abroad. He accomplished both objectives by leveraging Saudi oil wealth to cultivate a network of religious schools around the world that produced new generations of Muslim fighters for the battlefields in Afghanistan and beyond.

In a joint effort to defeat the Soviets, Washington supplied weapons to the *mujahideen* in Afghanistan.[42] As these fighters scored successes against the Soviet army, Congress expanded its funding for the weapons program, which the Saudis matched dollar for dollar.[43]

By some estimates, between 175,000 and 250,000 *mujahideen* fought in Afghanistan during the war.[44] The Arab contingent of fighters included roughly 5,000 Saudis, 3,000 Algerians, 3,000 Yemenis, 2,000 Egyptians, and scores of others from Tunisia, Iraq, Libya, and Jordan.[45] And though U.S. intelligence undoubtedly observed the effects of religious indoctrination on the *mujahideen*, the CIA never threatened to stop supplying them with weapons.

After the Soviet withdrawal from Afghanistan in 1989, many Saudi fighters returned home as war heroes. A sense of invincibility pervaded these "Afghan Arabs."[46] Perhaps no one demonstrated that sense more than Osama bin Laden, the wealthy son of a Saudi building magnate.

Bin Laden left his life of luxury in Saudi Arabia to become a guerrilla fighter in 1979, when the Soviet Union invaded Afghanistan. Inspired by an influential Palestinian professor and Muslim Brotherhood leader named Abdullah Azzam, bin Laden founded *Maktab al-Khidamat* (Services Office, or MAK) in 1984, and received financial donations from Saudi intelligence, the Saudi Red Crescent, and the MWL.[47] With that funding, MAK recruited thousands of *mujahideen*, financed their travel to Afghanistan, and trained them in guerrilla tactics and operations.[48] After the Soviet defeat, MAK became the core of the al-Qaeda network. Its fighters returned to their countries of origin with the intent to create new, local Islamist militant groups.

42 Charles C. Cogan, "Partners in Time: The CIA and Afghanistan Since 1979," *World Policy Journal*, Vol. 10, No. 2, Summer 1993, p. 76, www.jstor.org/discover/10.2307/40209308?uid=3739584&uid=2129&uid=2&uid=70&uid=4&uid=3739256&sid=21100651139186. (Requires JSTOR account to access)

43 Coll, *Ghost Wars*, pp. 81-106.

44 Peter Bergen, *Holy War, Inc.: Inside the Secret World of Osama bin Laden*, (NY: Free Press, 2001), p. 55.

45 Richard Engel, "Inside Al-Qaeda: A Window into the World of Militant Islam and the Afghan Alumni," *Jane's International Security*, September 28, 2001, republished at www.freerepublic.com/focus/f-news/559098/posts.

46 Raymond Ibrahim, "Al-Qaeda," *The World Almanac of Islamism*, http://almanac.afpc.org/al-qaeda.

47 Gold, *Hatred's Kingdom*, pp. 128-9.

48 *The 9/11 Commission Report*, p. 55.

When Saddam Hussein's Iraqi army invaded Kuwait in 1990, bin Laden "proposed to the Saudi monarchy that he summon *mujahideen* for a *jihad* to retake Kuwait. He was rebuffed, and the Saudis joined the U.S.-led coalition."[49] Shortly thereafter, bin Laden publicly challenged the Saudi regime, convinced that it did not rule Saudi Arabia in a manner consistent with Islamic law. He recorded speeches decrying the regime, and distributed them throughout the country.[50] As bin Laden later said, the government "betrayed the *ummah* [worldwide Muslim community] and joined the *kuffar* [infidels], assisting and helping them against Muslims."[51]

By April 1991, under pressure from the Saudi security services, bin Laden, his family, and an estimated 300 to 480 dedicated *jihadi* cadres left for Sudan.[52] It was there that bin Laden created his organization, which the Saudis disavowed, but was nonetheless an outgrowth of Wahhabi ideology. Under pressure from Washington, Khartoum reportedly tried to cut a deal with the Saudis in 1995 to extradite him, but it fell through. Finally, in 1996, bin Laden left for Afghanistan.[53]

From 1996 through 2001, conflicts in the Muslim world (including in Chechnya, Kosovo, and the Palestinian Territories) allowed bin Laden to attract a wave of Saudis to al-Qaeda's training camps in Afghanistan.[54] U.S. intelligence agencies estimated that between 10,000 and 20,000 fighters trained in bin Laden's camps during that time. As al-Qaeda developed into a deadly terrorist network, Saudi individuals and organizations funded its operations. Specifically, *The 9/11 Report* found that Saudi and Gulf financiers funneled money to jihadists in Afghanistan, and later to al-Qaeda, through an informal financial network of charities and non-governmental organizations, known as the "Golden Chain."[55]

The Fight against Jihadism in Saudi Arabia

The Saudi-U.S. relationship came under severe strain after September 11, 2001, as Americans learned that 15 of the 19 hijackers were Saudis and followers

49 Ibid., p. 57.

50 Bergen, *Holy War, Inc.*, pp. 77-78.

51 News Hour with Jim Lehrer, "Bin Laden's Fatwa," PBS, www.pbs.org/newshour/terrorism/international/fatwa_1996.html.

52 Yonah Alexander & Michael Swetnam, *Usama bin Laden's al-Qaida: Profile of a Terrorist Network*, (NY: Transnational Publishers, 2001), p. 38.

53 John-Thor Dahlburg & Alex Rodriguez, "Osama bin Laden, Born to Privilege, Dies a Pariah," *The Los Angeles Times*, May 2, 2011, http://articles.latimes.com/2011/may/02/local/la-me-osama-bin-laden-20110502-4.

54 Thomas Hegghammer, "Terrorist Recruitment and Radicalization in Saudi Arabia," *Middle East Policy*, Vol. 13, Issue 4, December 2006, http://chenry.webhost.utexas.edu/usme/2007/Saudi-Terrorist_Recruitmen_87543a.pdf.

55 *The 9/11 Commission Report*, pp. 55 & 67.

of bin Laden. Authorities raided, shut down, or froze the assets of nearly 50 Islamic institutions, most of them funded by Saudi Arabia, because of links to terrorist activities. Those organizations included the Muslim World League, World Assembly of Muslim Youth, SAAR Foundation, and the School of Islamic and Social Sciences.[56] Under fire, the Saudis took tentative steps to stem the flow of those toxic funds. For example, the Saudi and U.S. governments jointly designated several branches of the Al Haramain Foundation as financiers of terrorism under UN Security Council Resolution 1267.[57]

But the Saudi government was slow to implement a comprehensive counterterrorism strategy, and soon paid for its hesitation in blood. In early 2002, between 300 and 1,000 Saudi and foreign al-Qaeda members returned to the kingdom after the U.S. invasion of Taliban-ruled Afghanistan.[58] They formed independent cells and prepared for local operations by stockpiling weapons, renting safe houses, setting up training camps, and recruiting other "Afghan Arabs."[59]

Violence erupted on the streets of Saudi Arabia in 2003 and 2004, as al-Qaeda in the Arabian Peninsula (AQAP) launched more than 30 attacks inside the kingdom, killing at least 91 foreign nationals and Saudi civilians and 41 security officers, as well as injuring nearly 730 people.[60] The group assassinated senior officers in the Ministry of Interior, killed nine people at the U.S. consulate in Jeddah in 2004, and targeted the kingdom's largest oil processing facility at Abqaiq.[61]

A small cohort of clerics in the kingdom endorsed the campaign, including Hamud ibn Uqla al-Shuaibi, Abdullah ibn al-Jibreen, Nasir al-Fahd, Ali al-Khudeir, and Ahmed al-Khalidi (the latter three were arrested in the fall of 2003 and later renounced their support for militancy on television).[62] They propagated messages via the internet, accusing the Saudi government of subservience to infidels, and therefore deeming it a legitimate target for *jihad*.[63]

56 Alexiev, "The End of an Alliance."

57 "Combating Terrorism: U.S. Agencies Report Progress Countering Terrorism and Its Financing in Saudi Arabia, but Continued Focus on Counter Terrorism Financing Efforts Needed," U.S. Government Accountability Office, September 2009, p. 9, www.gao.gov/new.items/d09883.pdf.

58 Hegghammer, "Terrorist Recruitment and Radicalization in Saudi Arabia," p. 42.

59 Thomas Hegghammer, "Islamist Violence and Regime Stability in Saudi Arabia," *International Affairs*, Vol. 84, No. 4, 2008, http://hegghammer.com/_files/Hegghammer_-_Islamist_violence_and_regime_stability_in_Saudi_Arabia.pdf.

60 Angel Rabasa et al., *Deradicalizing Islamist Extremists*, (Santa Monica, CA: RAND Corporation, 2008), p. 56, www.rand.org/pubs/monographs/2010/RAND_MG1053.pdf.

61 Bruce Riedel and Bilal Y. Saab, "Al Qaeda's Third Front: Saudi Arabia," *Washington Quarterly*, Spring 2008, p. 38, www.twq.com/08spring/docs/08spring_riedel.pdf.

62 Toby Craig Jones, "The Clerics, the Sahwa and the Saudi State," p. 4.

63 Commins, "The Jihadi Factor in Wahhabi Islam," p. 13.

The regime downplayed their views as "deviant," yet their thinking was undeniably molded by the Saudi system. Al-Shuaibi, for example, came from the Wahhabi heartland town of Buraida, studied under Grand Muftis Muhammad ibn Ibrahim Al al-Sheikh and Abdulaziz Abdullah ibn Baz, and taught several prominent clerics, including current Grand Mufti Abdulaziz Al al-Sheikh.[64] For his part, al-Jibreen formerly worked within the official religious establishment at the Permanent Committee for Research and Ifta (issuing *fatawa*).[65]

The Crackdown

The Saudis launched an unprecedented crackdown, designed to root out terror finance and radicalism from the kingdom. The approach, according to the Saudi government, focused on "men, money, and mindset."[66] Between 2003 and 2008, Saudi security forces broke up al-Qaeda cells and arrested or killed militants suspected of planning attacks. Officials from the Ministry of Islamic Affairs monitored tens of thousands of the country's approximately 70,000 mosques, in addition to schools and websites.[67]

The government also launched a de-radicalization program designed to combat "deviant" ideologies, a term it prefers over "extremists" or "terrorists."[68] Its overarching "soft" counterterrorism strategy is known as PRAC, or Prevention, Rehabilitation, and Aftercare.[69] Largely administered by the Ministry of Interior, the Saudi program aims to: educate the Saudi population about the dangers of extremism; de-radicalize and re-educate extremists; and reintegrate individuals who completed the rehabilitation phase.[70] While recidivism rates are fuzzy and undoubtedly higher than reported,[71] it is still remarkable that the Saudi regime began battling the ideology it had promoted for years.

In the end, the counter-terror finance campaign was perhaps the most impressive

64 For Hamud ibn Uqla al-Shuaibi's personal website, see www.al-oglaa.com.

65 For Abdullah ibn al-Jibreen's personal website, see http://ibn-jebreen.com/?t=books&cat=200&book=75&toc=4754&page=4280&subid=.

66 "Initiatives and Actions to Combat Terrorism," (Washington, DC: Royal Embassy of Saudi Arabia, 2011), www.saudiembassy.net/files/PDF/Reports/Counterterrorism.pdf.

67 "Combating Terrorism," U.S. Government Accountability Office, p. 26.

68 Rabasa et al., *Deradicalizing Islamist Extremists*, pp. 57-77.

69 John Horgan & Kurt Braddock, "Rehabilitating the Terrorists? Challenges in Assessing the Effectiveness of De-radicalization Programs," *Terrorism and Political Violence*, Vol. 22, 2010, pp. 267-291, www.start.umd.edu/start/publications/Derad.pdf.

70 Christopher Boucek, "Saudi Arabia's 'Soft' Counterterrorism Strategy: Prevention, Rehabilitation, and Aftercare," Carnegie Endowment for International Peace, September 2008, http://carnegieendowment.org/files/cp97_boucek_saudi_final.pdf.

71 Rob L. Wagner, "For Saudi Terror Suspects, a Legal Fog," *The Jerusalem Post*, October 19, 2011, www.jpost.com/Features/InThespotlight/Article.aspx?id=242421&R=R44.

centerpiece of the new Saudi policy. As late as 2007, former Undersecretary of the Treasury for Terrorism and Financial Intelligence Stuart Levey said, "If I could somehow snap my fingers and cut off the funding from one country, it would be Saudi Arabia."[72] But in recent years, Treasury officials admit that U.S.-Saudi cooperation on terror finance found its groove. As one former official who worked very closely on this issue stated, "To be sure, it's a different atmosphere. There is much more political will in Saudi on [this] issue than before."[73]

Still, while the Saudis largely cut funding to al-Qaeda, considerable funds continue to flow to other jihadist organizations. On May 22, 2011, the Pakistani newspaper *Dawn* reported that nearly $100 million in annual financial support for Salafi Deobandi and Ahl-i-Hadith clerics in southern Punjab originated in Saudi Arabia and the UAE. To find young subjects for martyrdom operations, the organizations targeted families with multiple children and severe financial difficulties, initially under the pretense of charity. Clerics indoctrinated the children, while teachers assessed their proclivity "to engage in violence and acceptance of jihadi culture." In exchange for each child, the organizations doled out average cash payments of $6,500.[74]

But what of the problems associated with internet radicalization emanating from Saudi Arabia? Has *jihadi* messaging continued to plague Saudi Arabia? Or has it waned as a result of the Saudi authorities' efforts?

The Foundation for Defense of Democracies (FDD) commissioned a study in January 2011 to examine the Saudi clerical presence online, and the extent to which clerics and their followers promote Wahhabi ideology. A decade after the September 11 attacks, and a decade after the worst crisis in U.S.-Saudi relations, FDD sought to learn: Is Saudi-sponsored radicalization still a problem online?

72 Brian Ross, "U.S.: Saudis Still Filling Al Qaeda's Coffers," ABC News, September 11, 2007, http://abcnews.go.com/blogs/headlines/2007/09/us-saudis-still/.

73 Jonathan Schanzer, "Saudi Arabia's Terror Finance Problem," *The Weekly Standard*, September 7, 2011, www.weeklystandard.com/blogs/saudi-arabia-s-terror-finance-problem_592744.html.

74 Qurat ul ain Siddiqui, "Saudi Arabia, UAE Financing Extremism in South Punjab," *Dawn*, May 22, 2011, www.dawn.com/2011/05/22/saudi-arabia-uae-financing-extremism-in-south-punjab.html.

The Study

To understand how Saudi clerics and their followers use the internet to express and disseminate religious ideas, FDD commissioned ConStrat. The company surveyed online content that Saudi clerics posted themselves, content that generally referenced the Saudi clerical establishment, or content that referenced any of the Saudi clerics by name.

During the six-month period, internet users in Egypt posted the lion's share of content that referenced Saudi clerics, with 29,808 entries. To a certain extent, this is a matter of simple math. Egyptian internet users vastly outnumber those in Saudi Arabia. The Egyptian government reported in February 2011 that the number of internet users in the country was 23.51 million.[1] In comparison, a report by the UN High Commissioner for Refugees listed the number of internet users in Saudi Arabia at 11.2 million.[2]

However, the main reason for the relative dearth of Saudi internet activity is that the kingdom has a high level of censorship. In January 2008, the Saudi Ministry of Culture and Information enacted new laws restricting the use of technology.[3] Perpetrators could receive long prison terms and harsh fines for:

- Anything contravening a fundamental principle or legislation, or infringing the sanctity of Islam and its [*Shari'ah*], or breaching public decency;
- Anything contrary to the state or its system;
- Reports or news damaging to the Saudi Arabian armed forces, without the approval of the competent authorities;
- Anything damaging to the dignity of heads of states or heads of

1 "Egypt's MCIT: Egypt Has 23.51 Million Internet Users, 71.46 Million Mobile Subscribers, and 3972 ICT Companies," *Arab Crunch*, April 28, 2011, http://arabcrunch.com/2011/04/egypts-mcit-egypt-has-23-51-million-internet-users-71-46-million-mobile-subscribers-3972-ict-companies.html.

2 "Internet Entries 2011 – Saudi Arabia," *The United Nations High Commissioner for Refugees*, March 11, 2011, www.unhcr.org/refworld/country,,,,SAU,,4d82268d28,0.html.

3 "Saudi Arabia," *OpenNet Initiative*, August 6, 2009, http://opennet.net/research/profiles/saudi-arabia.

accredited diplomatic missions in the kingdom, or harms relations with those countries;

- Any false information ascribed to state officials or those of private or public domestic institutions and bodies, liable to cause them or their offices harm, or damage their integrity;
- The propagation of subversive ideas or the disruption of public order or disputes among citizens;
- Any slanderous or libelous material against individuals.[4]

On January 1, 2011, the Ministry of Culture enacted a new regulation that further restricted online media. The Executive Regulation for Electronic Publishing Activity required all news sites, discussion forums, mobile phone text messaging (and other mobile phone-based content), and email groups to obtain a government license. The regulation makes the necessary license available only to Saudis who also must be at least 20 years old and have a high school degree.[5] Thus, while Saudi Arabia has proportionally large internet accessibility in relation to other Arab states, government censorship limits usage significantly.[6]

However, these strict internet laws did not prevent clerics from being active online. Of particular interest to FDD was the extent to which Saudi clerics operate within the state's "red-lines."

ConStrat utilized its proprietary software to mine the internet for entries that could yield insight into the potential influence of Saudi clerics. Two ConStrat researchers with native Arabic language fluency analyzed Arabic data, while two other researchers with specialized academic and practical training in Arabic language and culture analyzed the English data.

In the first phase of this study, ConStrat analyzed hundreds of *tafseer* (religious commentary) and *fatawa* (religious opinions) from the personal websites of Saudi clerics, as well as other websites that publish their commentaries and opinions. In this phase, ConStrat's research yielded data on 75 sanctioned clerics and 19 unsanctioned clerics from Saudi Arabia. However, only 30 of these clerics maintained websites—20 in Arabic and 10 in English. These 30 clerics' websites published a total of 1,752 *fatawa* and *tafseer* in Arabic and 840

4 Chiara Bernardi, "Saudi Bloggers, Women's Issues and NGOs," *Arab Media & Society*, Issue 11, Summer 2010, www.arabmediasociety.com/?article=757.

5 "Saudi Arabia: Rescind New Online Restrictions," Human Rights Watch, January 7, 2011, www.hrw.org/news/2011/01/07/saudi-arabia-rescind-new-online-restrictions.

6 "The Internet in Arab Countries," *Al-Bab*, June 27, 2009, www.al-bab.com/media/internet.htm.

in English. From these comments and opinions, researchers randomly selected and coded more than 500 entries.

For the second part of the study, ConStrat used two software platforms to mine the social media environment to explore how Saudi clerics' messages disseminate. ConStrat's proprietary *VX* technology collected data from online message boards, more commonly known as forums. Researchers used the names of 69 prominent Saudi clerics, written in Arabic and Roman script (with varying spellings), to conduct key word searches of forums in both languages. The technology searched millions of forums (including password-protected forums), multiple times per day for relevant data. *VX* also identified the forums hosting the most discussions about Saudi clerics, and the *fatawa* forum users were discussing most often.

ConStrat also utilized the market research software *ALTERIAN SM2* to analyze Arabic and English mentions of Saudi clerics on social media platforms such as Twitter, Facebook, YouTube, and Blogger. *SM2*'s Social Media Warehouse contains data from more than 9 billion social media mentions, blogs, tweets, posts, images, and conversations. *SM2* continuously scans and indexes online conversations to add to this warehouse, and collects more than 40 million new results daily. This includes mainstream news sites, as well as message boards, Twitter, Plurk, Wikis, YouTube, Flickr, Ning, Facebook, and LinkedIn.

According to *SM2*, Twitter was the single most active social media platform for all Saudi clerics, with 84.29 percent of the total content by source. Though some clerics did not maintain Twitter accounts, "tweets" and "re-tweets" containing their *fatawa*, YouTube videos, and announcements about their activity were still common.

Relative to their Arabic-speaking counterparts, English social media users were less interested in the clerics. For perspective, English users mentioned the three most popular clerics—sanctioned clerics Abdul Rahman al-Sudais and Saleh al-Fawzan, and unsanctioned cleric Salman al-Odah—590 times. By contrast, Arabic users mentioned the top clerics—sanctioned clerics Saleh al-Fawzan and Abdulaziz ibn Baz, along with Salman al-Odah—31,368 times.

In the end, ConStrat collected and coded data for nearly 40,000 entries from Arabic and English websites, forum threads, and social media posts.

Assigning Sentiment

One of the primary objectives of this study was to gauge *how* Saudi clerics and web-users talk about their ideas. To better understand the overall tone of the Saudi internet environment, ConStrat coded sentiment on a spectrum from moderate to militant.

We fully acknowledge that sentiment analysis—particularly one that describes religious figures and ideas as radical or moderate—is a sensitive and widely debated subject. Radical and moderate are relative terms. The goal was to broadly gauge sentiment as a means to collate and analyze it further. ConStrat's labels were created with the following contours.

MODERATE: Expresses pluralistic views and commitment to peaceful co-existence with all sects and religions; supports Muslim integration in non-Islamic societies and with modernity; and actively refutes teachings that support war against non-Muslims to spread Islam.

- *Example 1*: "It is the duty of citizens as well as governments to fight all forms of terrorism." (Grand Mufti Abdulaziz Al al-Sheikh)[7]
- *Example 2*: "Islam is established on the basis of coexistence between those who differ, even when those differences are in faith." (Salman al-Odah)[8]

NEUTRAL: Expresses views that are generally devoid of sentiment, but may demonstrate a desire to adhere to religious laws. These entries could be described as banal in nature.

- *Example 1*: Ruling on the steps of properly cleaning the body after engaging in sex with a spouse. (Abdullah ibn Muhammad ibn Ibrahim Al al-Sheikh)[9]
- *Example 2*: Ruling on instances when the bank pursues the co-signer and/or co-signee of a contract. The cleric said, "These are legal matters between you and the bank with which I do not interfere." (Saleh al-Fawzan)[10]

CONSERVATIVE: Expresses views that reflect rigidity on socio-economic matters; reluctance to adapt to modernity; encourages associating only with other Muslims; provides strict interpretation of *Quran* and *Shari'ah* in daily life.

- *Example 1:* "It is allowed for a woman to go see a male gynecologist if there are no female doctors available, but he [the doctor] shall not be with her [the patient] alone in the same room." (Abdullah ibn al-Qaoud)[11]

7 For the Grand Mufti's personal website, see www.mufti.af.org.sa.
8 http://en.islamtoday.net/node/1715.
9 www.saaid.net/Warathah/1/shaikh-m.htm.
10 www.alfawzan.af.org.sa/node/4305.
11 http://alqaoud.net/word.php?t=2.

- *Example 2:* "The Islamic State is allowed to set legislation to promote the public interests as long as that legislation does not contradict Islamic Law." (Permanent Committee for Research and Ifta)[12]

RADICAL: Expresses views that embrace disdain for other Muslims, religions, and cultures; demands dissociation of believers from "non-believers;" allows treachery (theft, deceit, etc.) against "non-believers."

- *Example 1*: Muslims should sever all relations with relatives who do not pray on a regular basis. Non-practitioners should be considered apostates. (Saleh al-Fawzan)[13]

- *Example 2*: "Muslims should only use force when they are compelled to...unless there is some cause on the part of the [infidels], such as their fighting the Muslims, or helping other enemies of the Muslims, or preventing them from following the path of Allah." (Muhammad al-Munajjid)[14]

MILITANT: Expresses views that endorse religious violence; supports *jihad* against "non-believers," including for the purpose of spreading Islam; and endorses killing for the sake of the Muslim nation (*ummah*).

- *Example 1*: "... *jihad* means fighting the infidels and the like. This is the duty of the people of the country that has been dominated or occupied by the infidels. The rest of the Muslims must assist and support them." (Salman al-Odah)[15]

- *Example 2*: "...Martyrdom operations...are legitimate in religion, a *jihad* for Allah, if the intention of the perpetrator is pure. They are one of the most successful means of *jihad* and effective means against the enemies of this religion." (Hamud ibn Uqla al-Shuaibi)[16]

While such labels were often useful in helping ConStrat identify moderate or radical sentiment, assigning such labels to define clerics proved impossible. Clerics who forwarded moderate statements also generated radical ones. For example, Abdul Rahman al-Sudais' message for Muslims to peacefully co-exist and uphold moderate Islamic teachings[17] stands in stark contrast to his calls for *takfeer* against

12 http://en.islamtoday.net/quesshow-118-575.htm.

13 www.alfawzan.af.org.sa/node/9116.

14 www.islam-qa.com/en/ref/21757.

15 www.islamtoday.net/salman/artshow-28-138541.htm.

16 www.al-oglaa.com/?section=subject&SubjectID=169.

17 "Al-Sudais Speaks about Challenges Facing Islam," *Arab News*, April 21, 2011, http://arabnews.com/ saudiarabia/article369488.ece.

Sufis, as well as his reference to Jews as "monkeys and pigs."[18] Likewise, Saleh al-Fawzan's ruling that the suicide bombing of a Coptic church in Alexandria, Egypt, was the work of Satan[19] is difficult to reconcile with his ruling that Muslim co-workers who do not pray are *kuffar* (infidels), and must be killed.[20]

Primarily, sentiment proved useful in flagging notable posts for the analyses in the chapters that follow.

Processing the Data

ConStrat also divided its data into seven thematic topics to ascertain what issues were on the minds of Saudi religious leaders and their audience:

ECONOMIC: Commentary related to issues such as the financial markets, banking, money lending, and domestic and international economic policies. Economics comprised 1 percent of the overall content in English, and 4 percent of the overall Arabic content. Most of the *fatawa* came in the form of questions and answers between web-users and clerics. One *fatwa* banned employment in the information technology field if the websites involved contain pictures or gender mixing. The *fatwa* also banned selling products that could lead to heresy, like "grapes to be used in wine" or "wood to be used for a cross."[21] Former Grand Mufti Muhammad ibn Ibrahim Al al-Sheikh also forbade "helping Christians celebrate Christmas" by selling greeting cards, gifts, and Christmas trees.[22]

SOCIAL: Commentary related to social issues such as women's rights, human rights, child rearing, crime, and punishment comprised 22 percent of the overall English content and 35 percent of the Arabic content. The Saudi ban on a woman's right to drive was the most discussed topic during the observation period.[23] Discussions also covered adultery[24] and Western customs.[25] The overall dominance of conservative and radical ideas reflected general resistance to social reforms by clerics and their followers. A handful of militant posts openly endorsed the use of violence against reformists.

18 R. Upadhyay, "Mecca Imam's Visit to India: Some Observations – Analysis," *Wordpress*, June 1, 2011, http://sunninews.wordpress.com/2011/06/02/mecca-imam%E2%80%99s-visit-to-india-some-observations-%E2%80%93-analysis/.

19 "Saudi Cleric Sees Devil behind Suicide Attacks," *The Daily Star*, January 8, 2011, www.dailystar.com.lb/News/Middle-East/Jan/08/Saudi-cleric-sees-devil-behind-suicide-attacks.ashx#axzz1WihSIApX.

20 www.alhilalclub.com/vb/showthread.php?t=268543.

21 www.neqashalhb.com/showthread.php?t=12182. (Login required; Accessed via VX on January 26, 2011)

22 www.mahaja.com/showthread.php?12388.

23 http://cn.last.fm/forum/23/_/717902?setlang=zh.

24 http://baytulaswad.blogspot.com/2011/06/does-marriage-of-adulterer-to.html.

25 www.friendswhisper.com/?p=540.

DAILY RELIGIOUS PRACTICE: Commentary related to how Muslims should practice their religion in their daily lives made up 29 percent of the overall English content, and 47 percent in Arabic. Most discussion focused on technicalities, such as the proper ways to perform ablution and prayer. One contentious issue that elicited more radical responses was worshipping at gravesites,[26] which is a practice Wahhabis oppose. Many requests for religious guidance came in the form of requests for clarification. For example, one ruling declared a woman's prayer invalid if she is wearing jewelry while praying.[27]

DOMESTIC POLITICS: Commentary related to the Saudi government and its policies made up 9 percent of the overall English language content, and 8 percent of Arabic content. Most of the conversations focused on unrest in Saudi Arabia during the protests of the regional "Arab Spring." While the March 11 protests were not widespread in the kingdom (the government warned of dire consequences in the event of unrest), questions surrounding reform prompted timid discussions about Saudi governance.

INTERNATIONAL POLITICS: Commentary related to foreign governments and international politics comprised 8 percent of the overall English content and 12 percent of the Arabic content. Most of the radical to conservative posts represent a hostile stance against the "Arab Spring." Notably, cleric Rabia al-Madkhali spoke out against protesting as a means to achieve reform, and branded revolutions as a "Leninist, Stalinist evil."[28] However, the commentary on clerical rulings varied greatly. "Arab Spring" supporters regarded democratic reforms as the best path toward freedom from dictatorships. Conversely, conservative and radical commentators aspired to revive the "age of glory" for the Muslim world by reinstating the rule of an Islamic Caliphate.[29]

SECTARIAN: Commentary related to other Muslim sects and other religions, including the practice of *takfeer* (whereby one Muslim excommunicates another) and violence against people of other sects and religions, made up 13 percent of the overall English content and 4 percent of the Arabic content. The more conservative

26 www.ummah.com/forum/showthread.php?296372- Visiting-graves-of-awliya.

27 www.almeshkat.net/vb/forumdisplay.php?f=2. (Thread no longer available; Accessed via VX on June 18, 2011)

28 http://forums.naseej.com/showthread.php?175845-%E5%E1-%C7%E1%CE%D1%E6%CC-%DD%ED-%C7%E1%E3%D9%C7%E5%D1%C7%CA-%E6-%C7%E1%DE%ED%C7%E3-%C8%C7%E1%CB%E6%D1%C7%CA-%E3%E4-%E3%E4%E5%CC-%C3%E5%E1-%C7%E1%D3%E4%C9-%E6-%C7%E1%CC%E3%C7%DA%C9%BF-%ED%CC%ED%C8-%C7%E1%DA%E1%C7%E3%C9-%C7%E1. (No longer live; Accessed on October 15 via VX)

29 www.ummah.com/forum/showthread.php?282608-Jihad-or-Khilafah-which-comes-1st.

and radical rhetoric focused on divisions between Sunni and Shi'a sects.[30] Almost all Sunni mentions of the Shi'a came in the form of insults. Many posts reflected hostility toward Iran, an enemy of the Saudi state.

MILITARY: Commentary related to military matters, particularly the U.S. presence in the region, and the issue of *jihad*, made up 16 percent of overall conversations in English, but just one percent in Arabic. One entry suggested that individuals can always practice *jihad* in defending against invasions, but expansionary or offensive *jihad* to establish more "space" for Islam must be carried out on direct orders from the Caliph.[31]

Broad Findings

FDD's study yielded five broad findings:

1. The tone of the conversations was mixed, but was generally marked by an absence of overt radicalization. Militant entries that explicitly endorsed or condoned violence accounted for a marginal number of the total entries scored. This does not, however, indicate an absence of intolerant or xenophobic positions. Conservative to radical entries represented roughly half of the English data, while in Arabic they represented about 75 percent.

2. Sanctioned clerics Saleh al-Fawzan and Abdulaziz ibn Baz, along with unsanctioned cleric Salman al-Odah, accounted for the bulk of Arabic data with 31,368 out of the total 38,525 posts related to one of them. They were also the most popular clerics on Twitter.

   In English, sanctioned clerics Abdul Rahman al-Sudais and Saleh al-Fawzan, along with Salman al-Odah, garnered approximately 50 percent of all social media mentions.

3. Message Boards/Forums carried the lion's share of the Arabic content related to Saudi clerics with 17,534 hits, or 45.51 percent of the total posts collected by *ALTERIAN*. Micro-blogs (Twitter, Plurk, Identi.ca, etc) accounted for 25 percent of total posts, while "Other Media," which included mainstream media sites, represented 23 percent.

4. In addition to social media outlets like Twitter, Facebook, and YouTube, Apple's iPhone, iPod touch, and iPad applications are gaining popularity among Saudi clerics to disseminate their messages. This phenomenon

30 http://islamicsystem.blogspot.com/2011/06/sectarian-card-shia-and-sunni-divisions.html.

31 www.ummah.com/forum/showthread.php?282608-Jihad-or-Khilafah-which-comes-1st.

contradicts the religious establishment's historical opposition to "corrupting" modern technology.

5. The volume of content related to Saudi clerics and their messages was significantly higher in Arabic than in English, suggesting that Saudi clerics have yet to fully penetrate American/Western society, at least in the online arena. However, English language web-users were far more concerned with militant issues than their Arabic-speaking counterparts; 16 percent of English conversations were military related, as opposed to just 1 percent of Arabic conversations.

Caveats

ConStrat's data helped to provide an interesting glimpse into the Saudi clerical establishment, its followers, and the broader Saudi online environment. Indeed, we believe that much can be learned from this data, particularly in light of Saudi society's insular nature. But the data derived from this study provides only one stream of information on Saudi society. It does not paint a full picture of how the Saudi religious establishment propagates its ideology, which includes outreach through radio, television, print media, mosque sermons, and textbooks. Moreover, even with ConStrat's advanced analytical tools, the internet is much too large to capture every mention of Saudi clerics.

Nevertheless, we believe that this study can help illuminate our understanding of Saudi Arabia, the way Wahhabi messages propagate on the internet, and how online data can be used as intelligence, particularly when consumed alongside other streams of information.

Responding to Arab Protests

On December 17, 2010, Tunisian street vendor Muhammad Bouazizi immolated himself in protest after the country's authorities confiscated his wares. This event sparked mass demonstrations that eventually deposed dictator Zine El Abidine Ben Ali on January 14, 2011.

Across the Middle East, the masses celebrated the drama in Tunisia as a step toward democracy. This was the first time that mass protests forced an Arab leader from office. By January 25, hundreds of thousands of protesters gathered in Egypt's Tahrir Square, also calling for the end of their regime. At the same time, protest movements sprouted in Jordan, Syria, and Yemen. Media commentators called it the "Arab Spring."

For the Saudis, concerned with preserving their autocratic state, this was the dead of winter.

Under intense domestic and international pressure, Egyptian dictator Hosni Mubarak stepped down on February 11. Days later, protests erupted in Benghazi, Libya, and ultimately mushroomed into a full-scale civil war that toppled Moammar al-Qadhafi in October. By March, sporadic protests in Syria evolved into an ongoing, full-scale uprising. Yemen's masses flooded the streets of Sana'a, and even Bahrain experienced spasms of unrest.

Saudi Arabia, however, remained relatively quiet during the zenith of the Arab protests. Small-scale demonstrations were reported in majority-Shi'a areas in the east, but calls for a massive revolution on March 11, organized by youth activists through Facebook, never materialized.

To some extent, the lackluster turnout was a surprise. The corruption, poverty, and lack of freedoms that set off uncontainable protests in neighboring Arab countries certainly exist in Saudi Arabia. And as French academic Stéphane Lacroix observed, "a new generation of young political activists is gaining increasing influence. They are connected through social networks, especially Facebook and Twitter, and count among their 'friends' numerous young Egyptian and Yemeni activists, whose revolutionary 'know-hows' they have been sharing in the last few months."[1]

But the Saudi regime enjoyed the support of its sanctioned clerics, who served as a counterweight to challenges facing the monarchy during the early months of the Arab protests.

On Self-Immolation

Shortly after Bouazizi's self-immolation, Saudi Grand Mufti Sheikh Abdulaziz Al al-Sheikh issued a *fatwa* ruling that Islam forbade self-immolation, describing it as a "heinous crime and a great calamity."[2]

Nasir al-Omar, the Saudi cleric who famously announced in 2006 that America was collapsing and the Islamic nation was entering "a great phase of *jihad*,"[3] issued a similar *fatwa* describing suicide as among the greatest sins in the *Quran* and *Sunnah*.[4]

Other clerics across the political spectrum also issued *fatawa* banning self-immolation. The online reactions, however, varied greatly. For example, one user on the English-language forum *pakpassion.net* noted, "The act of one such person in Tunisia sparked off a movement that pretty much toppled an autocratic government and sent shivers in the rest of the world—including the citadel of Islam [Saudi Arabia]." Another user wondered why this *fatwa* banning self-immolation did not apply to suicide bombers as well. Some charged that the clerics who banned self-immolation were puppets of the Saudi regime.[5]

Warnings from the Sanctioned Clerics

In March, media outlets and analysts speculated on the likelihood of the Arab protest movement reaching the kingdom. The Council of Senior Ulema responded by condemning all protests.

"The Council of Senior Ulema calls on everybody to exert every effort to increase solidarity, promote unity and warn against all causes giving rise to the opposite. In this connection, it stresses the importance of mutual advice, understanding, cooperation in righteousness and piety and forbidding sin and transgression and warns against injustice, evildoing and ingratitude."[6]

1 Stéphane Lacroix, "Saudi Islamists and the Potential for Protest," *Foreign Policy*, June 2, 2011, http://mideast.foreignpolicy.com/posts/2011/06/02/saudi_islamists_and_the_potential_for_protest&reason=0.

2 http://ksa.daralhayat.com/ksaarticle/225894.

3 www.kavkazcenter.com/eng/content/2006/05/05/4658.shtml.

4 http://almoslim.net/node/140211.

5 "Saudi Clerics Issue Fatwa Against Self Immolation," www.pakpassion.net/ppforum/showthread.php?p=3378492.

6 www.salafitalk.net/st/viewmessages.cfm?Forum=9&Topic=12255.

More important, the statement warned "against deviant intellectual and partisan tendencies as the people of this country are a single unit following the example of the *Salaf* [righteous ancestors], their successors and the old and contemporary Muslim *imams* when it come[s] to preserving unity."[7]

In essence, the Saudi government appealed to its citizens' Islamic sensibilities via the clerical establishment, without having to explicitly threaten them directly.

Crushing Skulls

Other clerics did threaten the citizens with violence. Saad al-Buraik's *fatwa*, broadcast on the Saudi-owned Al Majd TV, called for "smashing the skulls of those who organize demonstrations or take part in them."[8]

While the regime likely welcomed the statement, it stoked heated debates among some web-users on discussion forums. One user wrote: "Sons of Wahhab, their ill-intentions show on their faces. They deserve to be skinned and hanged from their beards that look like the hair on my aunt's donkey." In response, a user named Nasir al-Mubarak wrote: "...I heard you say sons of Wahhab, why don't you finish the word, you coward. It is Wahhabism, thank God, and I am one of them."[9]

The al-Buraik controversy caught the attention of *The New York Times*. Writing in "Room for Debate," Madawi al-Rasheed of Kings College, London ripped into the cleric. "Al-Buraik, an extremist but also a government loyalist, preaches hate against anybody who does not worship the Al-Saud, obey their orders, and maintain silence over their excesses," she said. "He is part of a prolific network of preachers embedded in state-funded institutions. His [*fatawa*] against Shi'a and Sunni activists are notorious. He is one of the extremists retained by the government to preach obedience at home and *jihad* abroad."

Al-Rasheed's observations extended beyond al-Buraik, and addressed the controversial role of clerics in Saudi Arabia. Specifically, she noted, "Like so many Saudi religious scholars, al-Buraik became excited at the prospect of *jihad* in Iraq against Americans and Shi'a. When jihadis brought bombs to Riyadh and Jeddah, he felt that they had misunderstood the message. *Jihad* outside Saudi Arabia is fine but don't bring it home. It may only be practiced at home against Westernized Saudi liberals who corrupt the purity of the nation or the Iranian fifth column, the Saudi Shi'a."[10]

---

7 Ibid.

8 http://aljazeeratalk.net/forum/showthread.php?s=eba60a156105ed071a8930bde0605a6f&p=3662105#post3662105. (Thread no longer available; Accessed via VX on March 17, 2011)

9 Ibid.

10 Madawi al-Rasheed, "Preachers of Hate As Loyal Subjects," *The New York Times*, March 14, 2011, www.nytimes.com/roomfordebate/2011/03/14/how-stable-is-saudi-arabia/preachers-of-hate-as-loyal-subjects.

Clerics without Borders

As Shi'a protesters threatened the stability of the pro-Saudi regime in Manama, 13 Saudi clerics issued a *fatwa* that warned of "illicit schemes in Bahrain." The clerics stated: "Any observer of the demonstrations in Bahrain would realize that they are outside the realm of demanding rights and fall under the circle of the implementation of suspicious schemes and agendas. This represents a forefront for a Safawi Magian [Zoroastrian] expansion that dreams of seizing the Arab Gulf and forming a Persian crescent."[11]

The *fatwa* sparked commentary from a number of users, who were divided over whether deploying Saudi forces to Bahrain would help calm or escalate the crisis.

In March, users discussed a *fatwa* by Abdul Rahman al-Barrak denouncing demonstrations in Yemen as *haram* (forbidden). "His eminence Sheikh Abdul Rahman al-Barrak considered the conflicts Yemen is witnessing, these days, to be a *fitna* [discord] that must be avoided... Shun turmoil, as most of those engaged in [demonstrations] are seeking mundane demands, rather than promoting the Word of Allah...bloodshed in this conflict is *haram*."[12]

Al-Barrak's statement was not roundly appreciated. One user stated, "You ought to leave the *fatwa* to the clerics of the country, as they are more knowledgeable about their own situation." Another, using a slightly more diplomatic tone, pleaded, "With all due respect to Sheikh al-Barrak, we would rather if he left this issue to the clerics of Yemen, God bless you."[13]

Al-Odah's Arab Spring

In early February, as the Egyptian uprising was in full swing, Salman al-Odah broke rank and expressed his support for the Egyptian demonstrators. According to a *Gulf News* report, al-Odah was "discussing the situation with friends on Facebook and Twitter," and cheering for genuine reform.[14] He apparently crossed the line. Days later, al-Odah issued a statement on Twitter informing his followers that Saudi authorities canceled his popular television show on MBC TV.[15] While he conspicuously avoided taking a stance on protests in the kingdom, al-Odah continued to criticize other regimes. One YouTube video posting, a mosque sermon issued in March, shows al-Odah challenging

11 www.nationalkuwait.com/vb/showthread.php?t=178129. (Access requires a password)

12 http://almoslim.net/node/143433.

13 Ibid.

14 Abdul Nabi Shaheen, "Two Prominent Clerics Want Mubarak to Go," *Gulf News*, February 9, 2011, http://gulfnews.com/news/gulf/saudi-arabia/two-prominent-clerics-want-mubarak-to-go-1.759043.

15 Fatima Sidiya, "Ministry Rejects Al-Odah's Allegation over Talk Show," *Arab News*, February 14, 2011, http://arabnews.com/saudiarabia/article262270.ece.

the legitimacy of the al-Qadhafi family to govern Libya.[16]

Al-Odah sparked another dramatic episode when, in early April, he chastised Turkish Prime Minister Recep Tayyip Erdogan's reluctance to support protesters in Libya and Syria. Al-Odah tweeted, "With all due respect, do not be a supporter to the criminals. It is the right of the Syrian and Libyan people to have the freedom your people have, so do not shake hands with those that are stained with the blood of its people." Al-Odah's website, *Islam Today*, hosted a vibrant discussion on this challenge to the Turkish head of state. One user asked al-Odah why his tweet was "not directed to the Gulf leaders during the three revolutions and now you are directing this message to Erdogan?" Others came to Erdogan's defense. One user asked, "Why don't we give Erdogan the benefit of the doubt and assume that he understands politics better than most others...?"[17]

Al-Odah continued to advocate for the Arab protesters into the early summer. In June, the cleric reminded his website's readers about South African leader Nelson Mandela, who "adopted peaceful disobedience and peaceful coexistence." Recalling that Robben Island Prison, where Mandela was incarcerated, became an historic monument, al-Odah mused that prisons in the Arab world could also become monuments for freedom. Speaking broadly about the protests across the region, he said, "I do not hide my optimism about what is happening..."[18]

Clerics vs. Autocrats

Other clerics also jumped in to denounce dictators. In late May, the Saudi-owned *al-Arabiya* carried Aidh al-Qarnee's claim that it was *fitna* (discord) for Yemeni President Ali Abdullah Saleh to remain in power. His statement contrasted sharply with Abdul Rahman al-Barrak's March declaration that Yemen's protesters were the cause of *fitna*. Al-Qarnee advised Saleh to resign immediately to stop the country's bloodshed, and urged the Yemeni people to accept Saleh's immediate resignation (if one were given) and forgive him.[19]

Debate over the statement varied, but most users disagreed with al-Qarnee. One noted, "Sheikh al-Qarnee's advice is not accurate here. The Yemeni president is better than others especially since his constitution is the Islamic *Shari'ah* and he does not fight the scholars." Another added, "I beg you Sheikh al-Qarnee, stay in mosques and only worry about prayer sermons." One other user praised him for voicing his disapproval, saying, "Our hero sheikh, I swear you are a hero. At least he said his advice and did not swallow his tongue and remain silent!!!"[20]

16 www.youtube.com/watch?v=Hq09gWzSdNA.

17 http://islamtoday.net/albasheer/artshow-12-148590.htm.

18 http://islamtoday.net/albasheer/artshow-12-151726.htm.

19 www.alarabiya.net/articles/2011/05/22/150092.html. (Link no longer available; Accessed May 25, 2011)

20 Ibid.

As the Arab protests intensified, a handful clerics who initially frowned upon regional protests appeared to experience a change of heart. Some broke ranks from their institutions, while others seemed to contradict themselves over time.

For example, in a clear break from the Council of Senior Ulema, Saleh al-Luhaidan called directly for Hosni Mubarak to step down, urging that he meet demonstrators' demands to preserve security and stability in Egypt. (By way of background, al-Luhaidan made headlines in 2005 for condoning *jihad* against American forces in Iraq.)[21]

Al-Luhaidan was not necessarily a cheerleader for the protesters, but rather an opponent of the Arab dictators trying to quell them. In late April, he issued a *fatwa* calling for *jihad* against the "atheist" Syrian government. The statement, first released on YouTube, was a reaction to the Syrian crackdowns that killed 270 protesters.[22] Al-Luhaidan boldly pronounced, "The Baath Party is fascist and malignant. It pretends to want to resurrect Arabs anew. However, Arabs have seen nothing but evil from them... I call on the Syrian people to be diligent in resisting the Syrian regime even if there are casualties."[23]

Nasir al-Omar, whose early *fatwa* against self-immolation served to temper the enthusiasm of protest movements, also shifted his stance. In June, amid continued unrest, he joined al-Qarnee in calling on the Yemeni regime to cease its "bloody crimes against defenseless people."[24] In July, the Association of Muslim Scholars, where al-Omar serves as secretary-general, condemned the "massacres" in Syria and called for the end of the Assad regime.[25]

Abdul Rahman al-Barrak, who denounced protests in Yemen, appeared to reverse his position on Egypt in late May. According to one *fatwa*, the protests in Egypt were "a testimony to God's power... Praise the Lord for what happened; which was needed for the people of Egypt and the evil is removed."[26]

Exactly what emboldened these clerics to reverse course and support the Arab protests is still unclear. However, the Saudi regime tolerated their support for the Arab street, apparently assured that its security was intact.

21 Lisa Myers, "More Evidence of Saudi Doubletalk?" MSNBC, April 26, 2005, www.msnbc.msn.com/id/7645118/.

22 www.sarayanews.com/object-article/view/id/65679&reason=0.

23 http://islamtoday.net/albasheer/artshow-12-149525.htm.

24 www.almoslim.net/node/147641?sms_ss=twitter%26at_xt=4ded07c85870cb5f,0&reason=0.

25 http://almoslim.net/node/149506&reason=0.

26 www.ajurry.com/vb/showthread.php?s=e0a50e83a3fa8b4edbbf31f95d04fbc8&p=56227#post56227.

Clerics under Fire

The online community was well aware of the clerics' hypocrisy. After demonstrations planned for March 11 failed to materialize in Saudi Arabia, one posting on almoslim.net noted that, "successive *fatawa* from the Council of Senior Ulema, and from other clerics in Saudi Arabia and its advocates had a clear impact—although not the only impact—in thwarting the demonstrations..." To this, one user lamented, "I wish the scholars used their influence to pressure the leaders to implement real, sweeping reforms instead of pressuring the poor nation."[27]

One user on the *al-Jazeera Talk* discussion board criticized King Abdullah's $37 billion financial package in February 2011 as an attempt to buy off his citizens.[28] "The king's decisions were a failed attempt to bribe the constituents and an admission to the pressure exerted by reform movements." Of particular note was his criticism of the *Ulema*. "The courtship of scholars and others belonging to the religious bodies," he noted, "...can only be explained as a reward for their support of the state's position and an encouragement to continue to do so in the face of any upcoming challenges."[29] One female user wrote, "Religion in Saudi serves the interests of the Al Saud, which means politicized religion."[30]

Among internet users, there was consensus that the Saudi clerical establishment was a bulwark for the regime during the "Arab Spring." Indeed, while a number of clerics shifted their views and challenged other regional leaders, they refrained from openly challenging the Saudi monarchy. As some clerics have learned, even they can pay a high price for dissent.

27 www.almoslim.net/node/143304.

28 Ulf Laessing, "Saudi Launches $37 Billion Benefit Plan," Reuters, March 1, 2011, www.reuters.com/article/2011/03/01/us-saudi-finmin-idUSTRE7204V320110301.

29 http://aljazeeratalk.net/forum/showthread.php?t=327235. (Thread no longer live; Accessed on March 30, 2011 via VX)

30 www.omaniaa.net/avb/showthread.php?t=251183. (Thread no longer live; Accessed on March 30, 2011 via VX)

The Saudi Struggle with Modernity

ConStrat culled many discussions on recent and past *fatawa* that aptly demonstrated Saudi Arabia's struggle with modernity. For example, one *fatwa* forbade giving flowers when visiting the sick, and furthermore prohibited the flower trade altogether.[1] A *fatwa* by Abdullah ibn al-Jibreen insisted that the Earth is flat and the sun revolves around it,[2] while Saleh al-Fawzan declared that open buffets are a heresy.[3]

Saudi Arabia, often diplomatically described as "deeply conservative," continues to struggle with Western ideas that are pulling the country—sometimes kicking and screaming—into the age of modernity. During our study, hundreds of *fatawa* and discussion threads confirmed this. These examples are a stark reminder that Wahhabism has not yet adapted to modern science, let alone the concepts of gender equality and tolerance that most countries embrace today.

Female Drivers

The question of female drivers in Saudi Arabia surfaced after the arrest of Manal al-Sharif, a woman who organized a bold campaign (by Saudi standards) to legalize female driving. Her cause was made famous by a YouTube video of her breaking the law and driving on Saudi streets.[4]

The debate was certainly not new to Saudi Arabia. In 1990, several dozen women held a public protest, calling for women to enjoy equal driving rights. As analyst Rachel Bronson noted, "The protests succeeded in capturing international attention, but also galvanized the Islamic opposition. The driving protest, and with it any hope for increased liberalization in Saudi society, was easily and effectively snuffed out. The same cannot be said for the increasingly radicalized Islamic opposition."[5] Indeed, the official clergy

1 www.humanf.org/vb/showthread.php?t=79246. (Accessed via VX on June 15, 2011)

2 www.djelfa.info/vb/showthread.php?p=6360171.

3 www.humanf.org/vb/showthread.php?t=79246. (Accessed via VX on June 15, 2011)

4 "Manal Al Sharif Driving in Saudi Arabia," YouTube, May 27, 2011, www.youtube.com/watch?v=sowNSH_W2r0.

5 Bronson, *Thicker Than Oil*, pp. 210-211.

played a leading role in banning women from driving, as the Council of Senior Ulema issued a *fatwa* prohibiting them from doing so.[6]

Online, some two decades later, the debate resurfaced. The issue sharply divided web-users, and conversations often escalated to name-calling. Surprisingly, both male and female bloggers were proportionally represented on both sides.[7]

Much of the conversation revolved around a statement by Deputy Minister of Internal Affairs Prince Ahmed ibn Abdulaziz, confirming that the ban "is still in effect" and those who "violate the ban will be severely punished."[8] Web-users cited former Grand Mufti ibn Baz's *fatwa* from 1991 to confirm their opposition to the "Westernization" of Saudi society.[9]

Then, Abdul Rahman al-Barrak, a blind cleric who is known to support gender segregation, wished death upon all women who seek to drive, and called for Manal al-Sharif to be imprisoned.[10] Al-Barrak described female drivers as, "women who open the gates of evil, seeking to westernize the country."[11]

But Aidh al-Qarnee challenged al-Barrak. In a post on Salman al-Odah's *Islam Today* website, al-Qarnee found "no evidence preventing women from driving a car," and explained that "this matter should be handled by a scholarly committee to be examined in order to avoid...controversy." Al-Qarnee disagreed that the kingdom would become like other Western nations, and highlighted drawbacks to preventing women from driving, "such as having to be alone in a car with the driver on the way to work or *souq* [market]."[12]

In December 2011, the Permanent Committee for Research and Ifta, one of the highest religious bodies in the kingdom, drafted a report on the potential impacts of repealing the driving ban. The report suggested that allowing women to drive would "provoke a surge in prostitution, pornography, homosexuality, and divorce," and further stated that within 10 years, there would be "no more virgins."[13] One woman, 34-year-old Shaima Jastaniya, was

6 "Women Driving Issue Needs No Fatwa: Saudi Cleric," *Al-Arabiya*, May 25, 2010, www.alarabiya.net/articles/2010/05/25/109562.html.

7 For some examples of the discussion, see: www.almeshkat.net/vb/showthread.php?t=100051 and http://noor-elislam.net/vb/showthread.php?t=13855.

8 http://awwamn.blogspot.com/2011/05/blog-post_5121.html.

9 www.traidnt.net/vb/traidnt1863772-14/#post16753988.

10 "Saudi Cleric Backs Gender Segregation with Fatwa," Reuters, February 9, 2010, http://in.reuters.com/article/2010/02/23/idINIndia-46408620100223?pageNumber=1&virtualBrandChannel=0&sp=true.

11 http://alanba.com.kw/AbsoluteNMNEW/templates/last2010.aspx?articleid=198634&zoneid=29.

12 Ibid.; See also: http://islamtoday.net/albasheer/artshow-12-151273.htm.

13 "Saudis Fear There Will Be 'No More Virgins' and People Will Turn Gay If Female Drive Ban Is Lifted," *The Daily Mail*, December 1, 2011, www.dailymail.co.uk/news/article-2068810/Saudis-fear-virgins-people-turn-gay-female-drive-ban-lifted.html.

sentenced to 10 lashes in September for defying the driving-ban, though King Abdullah later commuted her sentence.[14]

Sex Segregation

In January, more than 100 doctors and religious scholars called for the establishment of women-only hospitals in all Saudi cities in a report to the Saudi Shura Council and Ministry of Health. The report grew out of an October 2010 Facebook petition, "Pure Hospitals," calling for women-only hospitals, which enjoyed posthumous support from former Grand Muftis Muhammad ibn Ibrahim Al al-Sheikh and ibn Baz, who previously asserted that female students "suffer from mingling."[15]

Discussion forums buzzed about a petition signed by 56 influential Saudis requesting current Grand Mufti Abdulaziz Al al-Sheikh's endorsement of gender segregation in hospitals. According to the post, "One of the most important requests by our clerics and scholars in our good country was to establish hospitals reserved for men and others reserved for women, to have medical care and nursing of men by men; and medical care and nursing for women by women. To protect peoples' modesty and prevent the forbidden mixing..."[16]

Responses were largely positive. One user exclaimed, "Well Done! Enough with male doctors standing between the legs of a girl during labor!" Another asked, "Are you okay with male doctors looking at your wife's private parts?"[17]

But the question of segregation did not end with healthcare. In late May and early June, web forum users debated a new *fatwa* by the Council Senior of Ulema banning gender mixing at work.[18] Concerns stemmed from the fact that a woman cashier "meets with tens of men in a single day, talks to them, and hands things to them..." The CSU responded that a "Muslim woman should not work in a place where there is mixing with men. It is her duty to stay away from grouping with men and look for a job that is allowed [by Islam], which does not expose her to lust...if men lust after her it is *haram* [forbidden], and her employment by these companies is helping her commit a *haram* act."[19]

One website, *Noor al-Yaqeen*, even promoted gender separation in the virtual world. The site forbids females from interacting with clerics in the online forum "unless it is a case of dire emergency."[20]

14 Sam Jones, "Saudi Woman Driver Saved from Lashing by King Abdullah," *The Guardian*, September 29, 2011, www.guardian.co.uk/world/2011/sep/29/saudi-woman-lashing-king-abdullah.

15 Fatima Sidiya & MD Al-Sulami, "Debate on Gender Mixing in Hospitals Moves from Facebook to Shoura," *Arab News*, January 12, 2011, http://arabnews.com/saudiarabia/article233084.ece.

16 www.alsahanet.com/showthread.php?s=2b8dc9ffdd40f36518cd2d89a2d889ac&p=73966#post73966.

17 Ibid.

18 www.almeshkat.net/vb/showthread.php?t=100736.

19 www.coalles.com/vb/f-3/t-52787/.

20 www.noor-alyaqeen.com/vb/t20696/.

Notwithstanding all of the talk about segregating the sexes, Saudi laws banned female clerks from working in lingerie stores until the king issued a royal decree in early January 2012. In a society where men are given preference, and female workers are frowned upon, shopping for undergarments was decidedly awkward. As Ellen Knickmeyer wrote in *Foreign Policy* in June 2011, female consumers were forced to consult with "male clerks about cup sizes and overflowing muffin tops."[21] To put it mildly, the debate underscores the inherent challenges of a Saudi social system under strain.

Other Rulings on Women

In April, cleric Muhammad al-Arefe appeared on a talk show, and responded to an advice-seeking caller who knew a father who was molesting his daughter. Rather than calling for authorities to arrest the father, al-Arefe advised that, "The girl should not be left alone with her father nor should she wear provocative clothing around him."[22] One discussion thread surrounded a *fatwa* that justified "forcing" a wife in mourning to have sex with her husband in order to fulfill her "matrimonial duty."[23] Another ruling declared a woman's prayers invalid if she is wearing jewelry while praying.[24]

Some social media users debated Council of Senior Ulema member Saleh al-Fawzan's 2003 ruling that slavery is permitted in Islam. The blog *Maid Online* (now inactive) advocated on behalf of Indonesian domestic workers, and cited al-Fawzan's ruling in support of slavery with a graphic picture of an abused Indian maid in Saudi Arabia and stories of modern day slavery in the country.[25]

Broadly speaking, women are second-class citizens in Saudi Arabia, and many clerics frown upon attempts to change the system. Grand Mufti Abdulaziz Al al-Sheikh underscored that notion when he declared, "Proponents of women's emancipation" are "advocates of evil and misguidance."[26]

Women Bloggers and Internet Activists

While proponents of reform have ample reason to castigate Saudi Arabia's treatment of women, there are many female bloggers who defend the Saudi system and clerical rulings that support it. ConStrat flagged the following English language sites:

21 Ellen Knickmeyer, "In Saudi Arabia, An Undercover Revolution," *Foreign Policy*, June 27, 2011, www.foreignpolicy.com/articles/2011/06/27/in_saudi_arabia_an_undercover_revolution.

22 http://alanba.com.kw/AbsoluteNMNEW/templates/Aworld.aspx?articleid=189022&zoneid=194.

23 www.almeshkat.net/vb/showthread.php?t=96354.

24 www.almeshkat.net/vb/forumdisplay.php?f=2.

25 http://maid-online.blogspot.com/2011/06/slavery-and-destruction-of-islamic.html. (Blog has been removed)

26 http://almoslim.net/node/139995.

Dawah tu Salafiyyah Sisters Book Club (www.dtssbnyc.blogspot.com), run by women from New York City. The site caters to "females striving to learn their *deen* [religion] from the scholars past and present." The site posts *fatawa*, *Ahadith* (sayings of the Prophet), as well as audio recordings and books by Islamic scholars. The operators of the site also claim to be involved in offline activism, and have even established Salafi libraries at two correctional institutions.

Scottishsalafiyyah (www.scottishsalafiyyah.blogspot.com) is a blog run by a woman who teaches at a mosque in Dublin, Ireland.[27] The blog's editor, Umm Hamam as-Salafiyyah, explained that she is a Salafi Muslim who does not perform *takfeer* (excommunication) against any Muslim, except toward polytheists.

Nuha38317.blogspot (www.nuha38317.blogspot.com) is mostly a collection of *fatawa* and *tafseer*, as well as writings from the *Quran* and *Ahadith*. This site is very conservative, but explicitly denounces jihadism. It often cites Saudi clerics, including Saleh al-Fawzan, but avoids topics like *jihad* and *takfeer*.[28]

Nikaahplanner (www.nikaahplanner.worldpress.com) is a blog about Islamic marriage. The site offers advice for married women and those planning to wed. A *fatwa* section gives clerical guidance on marriage.[29]

ConStrat also found that some of the most active participants in the forums discussing Saudi clerics' rulings are women.

For example, the top author during the monitoring period was Zadi Ila Lah, a 21-year-old university student from Egypt who is very active on *forums.fatakat.com*. She identifies herself as a Salafist woman and her objective as "spreading the word of Allah." She writes about women's issues and endorses strict interpretation of religious text, referencing official Saudi clerics Muhammad ibn al-Othaimeen, Saleh al-Fawzan, and Grand Mufti Abdulaziz Al al-Sheikh. She believes that women should wear the *niqab* (full body veil), even if companies refuse to hire them because of it. She also stresses the need for gender separation in public arenas,[30] considers Christians and Jews to be "infidels," and argues that any Muslim who questions that opinion is an infidel.[31]

The second highest contributor during the study was Azhar Abdul Rahman, who posted on *forums.fatakat.com*. She also adheres to Salafi ideology and

27 The author can also be found on Facebook at www.facebook.com/ummhamam.

28 www.nuha38317.blogspot.com.

29 www.nikaahplanner.worldpress.com.

30 http://forums.fatakat.com/thread1696717-2#post40895077.

31 http://forums.fatakat.com/thread1657924#post39798285.

strictly endorses separation of sexes in public and wearing the veil at all times, even during encounters between brothers and sisters-in-law.[32]

This is not to say that all Saudi online activists support the state's interpretation of Islam. Eman al-Nafjan, a graduate student from Riyadh, runs the *Saudiwoman's Weblog*. Her blog contains several articles supporting cleric Ahmed al-Ghamdi, who spoke out against gender segregation, the *niqab*, and the ban on women driving in Saudi Arabia.[33]

Fatawa Concerning Children

In April, web forum discussant "Iraqiyya Ana" posted Abdul Rahman al-Samih's *fatwa* that lamented the "excesses and indulgences" in children's television shows, especially the "songs that include rhythm...applause and whistling!" Iraqiyya Ana warned that such shows would make "Muslim children similar to Christian and Jewish children, get rid of these poisonous channels and raise your children to love the Book of Allah and his *Sunnah*."[34]

There was also a question surrounding the video game Pokémon, based on long-standing and paranoid concerns that the game promotes knowledge of Jews and Christians and symbols of deviant religions. The ruling stated that the game was one of the ways the *kafir* (infidel) teaches Muslim children the "path of atheism" and Darwinism.[35]

Other discussions pointed to the late Muhammad ibn al-Othaimeen's *fatawa* forbidding students to learn the English language[36] and banning children's toys that have faces.[37]

In July, Saleh al-Fawzan made headlines in *The Wall Street Journal* for his ruling that fathers may arrange marriages for their daughters "even if they are in the cradle." Al-Fawzan issued the *fatwa* after the Ministry of Justice said that it would do more to regulate marriages between pre-pubescent girls and Saudi men.[38]

32 http://forums.fatakat.com/thread1705503#post41151885.

33 http://saudiwoman.wordpress.com/2010/04/25/the-man-of-the-hour/; http://saudiwoman.wordpress.com/2011/01/26/the-commision-for-the-promotion-of-virtue-and-prevention-of-vices/; http://saudiwoman.wordpress.com/2011/04/03/going-back-in-time/#comment-9062.

34 http://forum.rjeem.com/t100458.html.

35 www.al-oglaa.com/?section=subject&SubjectID=187.

36 www.humanf.org/vb/showthread.php?t=79246. (Accessed via VX on June 15, 2011)

37 www.neqashalhb.com/showthread.php?t=12182.

38 Angus McDowall & Summer Said, "Cleric Fights Saudi Bid to Ban Child Marriages," *The Wall Street Journal*, July 29, 2011, http://online.wsj.com/article/SB10001424053111903635604576472011907391364.html.

De-legitimization of Non-Muslims

Some of the clerical rulings on Christians and other religious groups not only underscore the Saudi struggle with adapting to modernity, but also draw attention to the hostility and suspicion that Saudi religious authorities and their followers hold toward non-Muslims.

For example, clerics deemed Mother's Day un-Islamic because it is a secular holiday.[39] Other clerics opposed helping Christians celebrate Christmas, and forbade Muslims from selling greeting cards, gifts, and Christmas trees.[40] Likewise, according to one clerical ruling, Muslim women should not wear white wedding dresses because they might imitate Christians or other *kuffar* (infidels).[41]

39 www.friendswhisper.com/?p=540.

40 www.mahaja.com/showthread.php?12388.

41 www.ibnothaimeen.com/all/noor/article_4768.shtml.

The Social Media Generation

Since the first days of radio and television broadcasts in Saudi Arabia, the *Ulema* have bristled at the very idea of contemporary mass communication in the kingdom. In 1963, the *Ulema* voiced their displeasure upon hearing a woman's voice on the radio. Two years later, the first public television broadcast precipitated an attack by Islamists on the station's office in Riyadh. The government appeased the *Ulema* by allotting the majority of programming to religious issues and imposing media restrictions that adhered to societal customs. For example, Saudi media refrained from printing women's photographs in newspapers, showing the consumption of alcohol, or discussing religion outside of the official Wahhabi agenda.[1]

The government maintained this uneasy and restrictive environment for three decades, but encountered new challenges when the internet arrived in 1994. At first, the regime minimized the challenge by only granting access to academic, medical, and research institutes. When containing it proved too difficult, the Saudis made the internet available to the wider public in 1999. Nevertheless, authorities maintained control by creating a centralized infrastructure through which all service providers connect.[2] This has created a system of pervasive and effective censorship, not to mention surveillance, by the Saudi Communications and Information Technology Commission (CITC).[3] In addition, as is the case with television and radio, the government is careful to assuage the fears of conservative elements within the kingdom by mandating that online material adhere to Saudi cultural and religious norms. The government further censors material that is either deemed immoral or critical of Wahhabi teachings.[4]

1 Commins, *The Wahhabi Mission and Saudi Arabia*, p. 111.

2 "Internet in Saudi Arabia," *Communications and Information Technology Commission* (*CITC*), 2011, www.internet.gov.sa/learn-the-web/guides/internet-in-saudi-arabia/view?set_language=en.

3 Joshua Teitelbaum, "Saudi Arabia Contends with the Social Media Challenge," Jerusalem Center for Public Affairs, February 8, 2011, www.jcpa.org/JCPA/Templates/ShowPage.asp?DBID=1&LNGID=1&TMID=111&FID=442&PID=0&IID=6006.

4 Abdulrahman A. Mirza, "Saudi Arabia and the Internet Technology," King Saud University College of Computer and Information Sciences, 1998, http://repository.ksu.edu.sa/jspui/bitstream/123456789/2402/1/Saudi%20Arabia%20and%20the%20Internet%20Technology.pdf.

But censoring in today's evolving internet environment is a not as simple as it was in the late 1990s. Whereas certain content (like pornography) is easy to censor because the subject matter is narrow and specific, sites like Facebook and Twitter offer users platforms to circulate diverse material that can be harder to classify.[5] The Saudi state adapted by monitoring this space for violators of the social contract, sometimes relying on its citizens to report offenders, then tracking down and deactivating their accounts. In one widely reported example from August 2009, Saudi activists Walid Abdul Khair and Khalid al-Nasser criticized Saudi governance and human rights abuses over Twitter, and the government promptly responded by blocking both of their accounts.[6]

In the future, Twitter might begin censoring the regime's most outspoken critics before the government has to. On January 26, 2012, Twitter announced that it would initiate country-specific "tweet" censorship. The company explained, "As we continue to grow internationally, we will enter countries that have different ideas about the contours of freedom of expression. Some differ so much from our ideas that we will not be able to exist there."[7] Saudi Arabia is likely one of those countries.

Clerics Take Their Outreach Online

Despite their opposition to the "morally hazardous" mass media, both sanctioned and unsanctioned clerics now take to the internet with zeal. Particularly, the unofficial clerics have leveraged Twitter, Facebook, YouTube, and iPhone apps to propel their global influence and reach.

The sanctioned *ulema* also maintain personal websites, conduct interviews on Saudi television, and disseminate videos via social media channels, making themselves relevant, if not popular, online. Indeed, ConStrat noted that three of the top five clerics by volume of mentions were state-sanctioned. Despite this trend, Grand Mufti Abdulaziz Al al-Sheikh is not a fan. In late January 2012, Al al-Sheikh described Twitter as a site where people, "issue [*fatawa*] without any knowledge...and to lie in a manner that brings fame to some."[8]

Notwithstanding the Grand Mufti's protests, the number of Twitter users in the Arab world exploded during the reporting period, thanks to the protests that began in Tunisia and spread to Egypt and beyond. But even before the regional unrest, Twitter was on the march in Saudi Arabia. During 2010 alone, Twitter

5 Teitelbaum, "Saudi Arabia Contends with the Social Media Challenge."

6 "Two Human Rights Activists' Twitter Pages Blocked," Reporters Without Borders, August 24, 2009, http://en.rsf.org/saudi-arabia-two-human-rights-activists-twitter-24-08-2009,34262.html.

7 "Tweets Still Must Flow," *Twitter Blog*, January 26, 2012, http://blog.twitter.com/2012/01/tweets-still-must-flow.html.

8 "Saudi Grand Mufti: Twitter Is Full of Lies," *The Jerusalem Post*, January 28, 2012, www.jpost.com/MiddleEast/Article.aspx?id=255501.

reported to the Saudi-owned, London-based daily, *Al-Sharq Al-Awsat*, that the number of Saudi tweeters increased 240 percent. While the global average rate of increase for daily tweets was 95 percent, the corresponding Saudi rate was 440 percent.[9] ConStrat's data confirmed this spike, particularly among clerics and their followers.

Al-Odah at the Top

Salman al-Odah, whom *Forbes Middle East* ranked number four on its top 100 list of Arab "Twitterati" in 2011, is chief among the clerics active on Twitter.[10] Al-Odah is a veritable social media superstar. Operating Twitter accounts in both Arabic and English, he reaches a global audience of more than 840,000 followers.[11] His Facebook pages are linked to his Twitter and YouTube accounts, as well as his website *Islam Today*, allowing him the potential to share his thoughts with millions of followers on any given day.[12] As of March 2012, al-Odah's Arabic Facebook page boasted more than 635,000 "likes."

The West may see a downside to al-Odah's popularity: In the early 1990s, he was said to have inspired Osama bin Laden. Often described as "fiery," al-Odah attacked the West and openly challenged the Islamic credentials of the Saudi monarchy. But some analysts say the popular cleric is different. For example, Ed Husain of the Council on Foreign Relations claims, "I follow Shaikh Salman on Arabic Twitter, and gone is the man who cites chapter and verse to incite young minds towards agitation. Now in his fifties, he is mild and mature. He tweets contemplative questions about love, compassion, spirituality, forgiveness, and humanity."[13]

Nonetheless, we should not forget where al-Odah once stood, and that he only moderated after serving a five-year prison term. As Husain concedes, "A country that stones adulterers, beheads murderers, and amputates the limbs of thieves was not sufficiently [*Shari'ah*]-compliant for him."[14]

Al-Odah still challenges the Wahhabi system today, albeit from a more liberal perspective. In February 2011, for example, he signed a petition titled "Toward a State of Rights and Institutions," which advocated for a transition to

9 Badr al-Qahtani, "Saudi Arabia: Twitter Use Skyrockets in 2010," *Al-Sharq Al-Awsat*, January 3, 2011, www.asharq-e.com/news.asp?section=5&id=23646.

10 For *Forbes Middle East*'s List, see www.forbesmiddleeast.com/arabic/ اكثر-100-شخصية-عربية-حضورا-على-تويتر/.

11 For Al-Odah's English Page, see http://twitter.com/Salman_Al_Odah; For Arabic, see http://twitter.com/salman_alodah.

12 For Al-Odah's English Page, see www.facebook.com/DrSalmanAlOadah; For Arabic, see www.facebook.com/SalmanAlodah.

13 Ed Husain, "Radical Turnaround in Saudi Arabia," *Council on Foreign Relations*, October 13, 2011, http://blogs.cfr.org/husain/2011/10/13/radical-turnaround-in-saudi-arabia/.

14 Ed Husain, "Saudi Advice to Egypt's Muslim Radicals," *Council on Foreign Relations*, October 14, 2011, http://blogs.cfr.org/husain/2011/10/14/saudi-advice-to-egypt%E2%80%99s-muslim-radicals/.

constitutional monarchy in Saudi Arabia, among other reforms.[15] Soon thereafter, the government cancelled his program on Saudi-owned MBC TV, prompting outraged followers to post hundreds of messages disparaging the network.[16]

Despite losing his program, al-Odah continues to support change in the Arab world. Al-Odah derided Arab governments over Twitter in June 2011, saying, "We don't expect anything from the Arabs regarding the massacres in Syria. How much blood will be shed until the world seriously intervenes?"[17] Then, in October, after Tunisia held its first elections since the overthrow of President Ben Ali, al-Odah wrote, "Tunisia reaps the first fruit of its glorious revolution. Congratulations great Tunisians. Soon we will see a great incident like this in Egypt and Libya and all their sister countries God willing."[18]

Second Place: Al-Arefe

According to the PR and marketing tool TweetLevel, which measures influence, popularity, engagement, and trust of Twitter users, the highest average scores among Saudi clerics, after al-Odah, belong to Muhammad al-Arefe and Aidh al-Qarnee.[19] Another similar platform, Klout, which measures online influence,[20] also attributed the highest scores to the same three clerics. In fact, a blog post on Wamda aggregated the top 100 Arabs on Twitter according to their Klout scores, and found that al-Odah, al-Arefe, and al-Qarnee all ranked in the top five.[21]

As of March 2012, al-Arefe's Twitter following was more than 1,044,000, significantly outnumbering al-Odah, while his Facebook retinue numbered far more than any other Saudi cleric, with more than 855,000 "likes."[22] This audience is strictly Arabic speaking; al-Arefe has not reached out to English-speakers. Nonetheless, his following is enormous. Throughout Ramadan 2011, the UAE telecom company, du, offered a daily program called "Ask the Sheikh," during which the cleric answered phone calls and responded to questions sent over Facebook from people seeking religious guidance.[23]

15 An electronic version of the petition is available on Facebook, www.facebook.com/notes/قلود-وحن-لاحقوق-و-لامؤسسات/نحو-دولة-لاحقوق-و-لامؤسسات/191724777528779; The petition is also referenced in this article: Abeer Allam, "Saudi Clerics Tap into Social Networks," *Financial Times*, July 6, 2011, www.ft.com/cms/s/0/8b9834c8-a7ff-11e0-afc2-00144feabdc0.html#axzz1bouqzAUj.

16 www.muslm.net/vb/showthread.php?t=421067#post2790798.

17 Salman al-Odah's English Twitter page is available at http://twitter.com/Salman_Al_Odah.

18 www.facebook.com/DrSalmanAlOadah.

19 Read TweetLevel's methodology here: http://tweetlevel.edelman.com/About.aspx.

20 Read Klout's methodology here: http://klout.com/corp/kscore.

21 Khaled El Ahmed, "The 100 Most Influential Arabs on Twitter," *Wamda*, January 24, 2012, www.wamda. com/2012/01/the-100-most-influential-arabs-on-twitter.

22 For Muhammad al-Arefe's Twitter page, see http://twitter.com/MohamadAlarefe; For his Facebook page, see www.facebook.com/3refe.

23 Derek Baldwin, "Corporates Offer Special Ramadan Services," *Gulf News*, August 8, 2011, http://gulfnews.com/business/features/corporates-offer-special-ramadan-services-1.848473.

The *Financial Times* claimed that al-Arefe, "with his piercing dark eyes and jet black hair and beard, has become a heart throb among his women followers."[24] The author of the *Saudiwoman's Weblog*, Eman al-Nafjan, described him as the "Brad Pitt of Sheikhdom...it almost seems like he has hypnotic super-powers. Even women will accept being told that they are less than men when it comes from his mouth."[25]

Western observers may view his influence negatively. Readily available videos of al-Arefe on YouTube show a troubling trend in his messaging. One video from September 2007, translated by MEMRI TV, shows the cleric and three men discussing spousal abuse by men and women. The cleric explained three ways a man should discipline his wife, saying that he should first admonish her, and if that doesn't work he should give her the silent treatment to show his anger. In the event that those two options fail, al-Arefe says the third option is to strike her. Specifying the nature of the "beatings," he points out that they should not be outwardly visible. "If he beats her, the beatings must be light and must not make her face ugly. He should beat her in some places where it will not cause any damage."[26]

Al-Arefe displayed his contempt for Shi'a Muslims during a Friday sermon in December 2009 at the al-Bawardi Mosque in Riyadh. In the video, he says, "the evil [Shi'a] continue to set traps, for monotheism and the *Sunna*[*h*]. They try to spread their false doctrine to the ignorant among the Sunnis...We shall not forget their treachery throughout history—in Muslim countries in general, and in Mecca and al-Madina in particular—or their attempts to ensnare the Country of the Two Holy Mosques (Saudi Arabia)."[27]

Finally, in yet another video from July 2010, al-Arefe endorsed violence against non-Muslims. "Devotion to jihad for the sake of Allah, and the desire to shed blood, to smash skulls, and to sever limbs for the sake of Allah and in defense of His religion, is, undoubtedly, an honor for the believer...Allah said that if a man fights the infidels, the infidels will be unable to prepare to fight (the Muslims)."[28]

Third Place: Al-Qarnee

Aidh al-Qarnee was the third most influential cleric on Twitter, boasting more

24 Allam, "Saudi Clerics Tap into Social Networks."

25 Eman al-Nafjan, "Prominent Saudis: Sheikh Mohammed Al Arefe," *Saudiwoman's Weblog*, September 13, 2008, http://saudiwoman.me/2008/09/13/prominent-saudis-sheikh-mohammed-al-arefe/.

26 www.youtube.com/watch?v=PJGjC1rsQXs&feature=player_embedded#!.

27 "Saudi Cleric Muhammad Al-Arifi Exposes Shiites and Their History-Affairs," YouTube, November 7, 2010, www.youtube.com/watch?v=3651za7DBN0&feature=related.

28 "Islam – Sheikh Arifi Kill Christians," YouTube, March 11, 2011, www.youtube.com/watch?feature=endscreen&NR=1&v=cQvkEzH4SQo.

than 750,000 followers as of March 2012.[29] Al-Qarnee is a mainstream Saudi cleric who writes weekly opinion editorials for *Al-Sharq Al-Awsat*, one of the most widely read Arabic dailies. However, al-Qarnee lacks the overall social media sophistication of his peers al-Odah and al-Arefe. While they each have well over half a million Facebook fans, al-Qarnee's Facebook page received just over 123,000 "likes" at the time of this writing.[30] One year after his YouTube channel debuted on January 24, 2011, followers viewed his uploaded videos more than 580,000 times.[31] By comparison, during nearly the same period, al-Arefe's followers viewed his uploaded videos a staggering 4.6 million times.[32]

Al-Qarnee's influence should also concern the West. In April 2010, he faced accusations of laundering money for the Muslim Brotherhood.[33] Furthermore, he is a known supporter of Hamas.[34]

Tops on Twitter

According to ConStrat, the top five clerics on Twitter by volume of mentions in Arabic were Salman al-Odah (profiled above), former Grand Mufti ibn Baz, Saleh al-Fawzan, Saleh al-Luhaidan, and Safar al-Hawali. Notably, three of the top five clerics are members of the sanctioned establishment; al-Odah and al-Hawali are the exceptions. This is impressive because *none* of the establishment clerics maintain Twitter or Facebook profiles. Thus, their opinions and rulings disseminate organically. Remarkably, ibn Baz's influence continues to reverberate beyond the grave, as hardliners and followers still cite his *fatawa* as justification for subjugating women, among other things.[35]

Most of Saleh al-Fawzan's Twitter hits reflected Arabic-speaking users' interest in his *fatwa* on the Arab protest movements, as well as a previous *fatwa* in which he determined that a co-worker who does not pray is an apostate and should be killed.[36] As noted earlier, al-Fawzan supported child marriage[37] and contended that slavery is a legal aspect of Islam.[38]

29 Aidh al-Qarnee's Twitter page can be accessed at https://twitter.com/Dr_alqarnee.

30 Aidh al-Qarnee's Facebook page can be accessed at www.facebook.com/dralqarnee?sk=wall.

31 Aidh al-Qarnee's YouTube channel can be accessed at www.youtube.com/user/drqarnee.

32 Muhammad al-Arefe's YouTube channel can be accessed at www.youtube.com/AlarefeTV.

33 www.alarabiya.net/articles/2010/04/22/106602.html.

34 "Shaykh Aed Al Qarni – Jihad, the Path to Victory!" YouTube, September 5, 2009, www.youtube.com/watch?v=wrEEu-fjzqk&feature=related.

35 "Saudi Disillusionment with the Religious Establishment," *Saudiwoman's Weblog*, July 20, 2010, http://saudiwoman.me/2010/07/20/saudi-disillusionment-with-the-religious-establishment/.

36 www.alhilalclub.com/vb/showthread.php?t=268543.

37 McDowall & Said, "Cleric Fights Saudi Bid to Ban Child Marriages."

38 "Saudi Sheik: 'Slavery Is A Part of Islam'," *World Net Daily*, November 10, 2003, www.wnd.com/?pageId=21700.

Saleh al-Luhaidan, a Council of Senior Ulema member, attracted commentary for denying that he issued a *fatwa* in support of Muammar al-Qadhafi, and for calling on Egyptian President Hosni Mubarak to step down in February 2011.[39] As noted earlier, al-Luhaidan exhorted co-religionists to kill owners of television networks that broadcast "immoral" material,[40] and openly encouraged Saudis to fight Americans in Iraq in 2005.[41]

As for Safar al-Hawali, he and al-Odah were the two figureheads synonymous with the *Sahwa* (awakening) movement that challenged the Saudi government during the early 1990s. Owing to the significant body of literature on the *Sahwa*, al-Hawali remains extremely well known. While he has tempered his rhetoric against the Saudi state, he continues to preach hatred and violence against Israel.[42]

Apple Applications

Another development that sharply contradicts the notion that the clerics despise modern technology is that a number of them now leverage Apple products. That would seemingly conflict with their ascetic version of Islam, yet Salman al-Odah proclaimed on his Facebook page that the merger of Islam and Apple products is a "remarkable friendship and brotherly relationship: The Qur'an was in her hand above the iPad...pure originality preserving the identity and keeping pace with the developing world." ("Her" identity is unknown.)

As of this writing, users can easily access iPhone, iPod touch, and iPad apps from their favorite clerics. For example, iTunes offers fans of al-Odah a free application, complete with articles, sound clips, and photos, as well as links to his Twitter, Facebook, and YouTube pages. The same app includes articles written about him and a direct link to his email address.[43]

Unsanctioned cleric Muhammad al-Munajjid, who ranked fourth overall among clerics on Twitter according to TweetLevel and Klout, maintains an equally impressive product.[44] The Zad Group offers a free app for al-Munajjid's website,

39 For al-Luhaidan's denial of support for Muammar al-Qadhafi, see www.ebnmasr.net/forum/t126704-4.html#post1484772; His call for Mubarak to step down can be found at www.sharesgate.com/vb/t67874.html#post705153.

40 Robert F. Worth, "Arab TV Tests Societies' Limits With Depictions of Sex and Equality," *The New York Times*, September 26, 2008, www.nytimes.com/2008/09/27/world/middleeast/27beirut.html.

41 Myers, "More Evidence of Saudi Doubletalk?"

42 For Safar al-Hawali's personal website, see www.alhawali.com/en/index.cfm?method=home.con&ContentId=6467.

43 Al-Odah's app is available at http://itunes.apple.com/us/app/id453331103?mt=8.

44 Al-Munajjid's app is available at http://itunes.apple.com/us/app/id428922481?mt=8.

Islam Question and Answer (*Islam Q&A*).[45] Available in 11 languages, including English, Arabic, Chinese, Russian, French, and Spanish, the application provides *fatawa* covering basic tenets of faith, etiquette and morals, Islamic history, and Islamic politics.

A number of al-Munajjid's messages are radical. In 2005, he stated that the deadly tsunami that hit Southeast Asia was punishment for Christians and sinners.[46] Under the section "Islamic Politics," the cleric rules that, "Democracy is a man-made system... Thus it is contrary to Islam, because rule is for Allah... and it is not permissible to give legislative rights to any human being, no matter who he is...Undoubtedly the democratic system is one of the modern forms of *shirk* [polytheism]."[47]

Regarding the Palestinian-Israeli conflict, al-Munajjid explains that, "The Palestinian issue is an Islamic issue...a solution cannot be reached in this matter unless it is regarded as an Islamic issue and the Muslims cooperate to find a solution, and wage an Islamic *jihad* against the Jews..."[48]

Some of the official clerics also embrace apps, but theirs are not free. For one dollar apiece, app developer Rich Ltd. offers enthusiasts a selection of audio *fatawa*, lectures, and commentary from ibn Baz, Muhammad ibn al-Othaimeen, and Saleh al-Fawzan.[49]

Respecting the Red Lines

Social media is now clearly an acceptable form of *da'wa*, or Islamic outreach. Indeed, Saudi Grand Mufti Abdulaziz Al al-Sheikh proclaimed that the internet should be viewed as a useful tool to spread Islam.[50] And as clerics offer their opinions amid regional protests, it appears regional politics are not off limits—at least for now.

But challenges against the state are still not tolerated. In July 2011, cleric Yusuf al-Ahmed, a professor at Muhammad ibn Saud Islamic University, directly petitioned King Abdullah three times to release prisoners detained indefinitely. On July 7, al-Ahmed posted his final appeal on YouTube; the next day, the

45 Find the Zad Group website at www.zadgroup.net/.

46 www.youtube.com/watch?v=HVDbvkBS7Iw&feature=player_embedded#!.

47 For the *Islam Q&A* app, see http://itunes.apple.com/us/app/id426345035?mt=8; For the complete fatwa, see www.islam-qa.com/en/ref/107166/ruling%20on%20democracy.

48 For the complete *fatwa*, see www.islam-qa.com/en/ref/21977/solution%20to%20the%20palestin ian%20issue.

49 To view all apps developed by Rich Ltd., click "View More By This Developer" in the top right corner of this page http://itunes.apple.com/us/app/id447655845?mt=8.

50 www.almoslim.net/node/148822.

administrator of his Facebook and Twitter profiles (rumored to be his son) announced that Saudi authorities arrested al-Ahmed at his father's home in the Eastern Province town of Dammam.[51] As of this writing, according to his Facebook and Twitter pages, the cleric still awaits trial.

When it comes to online messaging, clerics and everyday Saudis typically have a good understanding of the existing laws and the state's unspoken social contract. Some test the red lines. Others remain well within bounds. But with the proliferation of new mass communication tools, there are bound to be more challenges ahead.

51 Yusuf al-Ahmed's Facebook page can be accessed at www.facebook.com/pages/168817473166914 د-يوسف-الأحمد-الصفحة-الرسمية-/; His Twitter page can be accessed at https://twitter.com/yusuf-alahmed; To read an account of al-Ahmed's arrest as reported by Human Rights Watch, see "Saudi Arabia: Free Islamic Scholar Who Criticized Ministry," Human Rights Watch, July 14, 2011, www.hrw.org/news/2011/07/14/saudi-arabia-free-islamic-scholar-who-criticized-ministry.

Bin Laden and Jihadism

ConStrat was five months into collection when President Obama announced on May 1, 2011 that the United States assassinated Osama bin Laden in Abbottabad, Pakistan.[1] Not surprisingly, the Saudi online community was crackling with emotion. While many mourned his loss, many others viewed bin Laden's demise as a triumphant moment. Underlying all of the responses was a sense that, nearly a decade after the September 11 attacks, the ideology that inspired bin Laden and his network is deeply rooted.

Soon after the news broke, as celebrations in the U.S. flooded the wires, Salman al-Odah weighed in on his Facebook page. "The current joy of the greatest country after killing one person whom they have been pursuing for ten years, is a sign of weakness and incompetence, not a sign of strength and competence. The US dreamt of finding him alive, but God willed otherwise."[2]

He continued: "We disagree with [bin Laden's] actions, and call for mercy and forgiveness on his soul. However, ideas do not end by the demise of their owners; these ideas are resisted by ideas, by spreading justice, and correcting mistakes."[3] In this way, the unsanctioned cleric warned that the war is far from over.

Al-Odah previously inspired bin Laden in the 1990s, but he now vociferously opposes al-Qaeda's tactics. In 2007, al-Odah challenged the al-Qaeda leader, "How much blood has been spilt? Will you be happy to meet God Almighty carrying the burden...on your back?[4] After bin Laden's demise, numerous media outlets pointed to the cleric's condemnation of bin Laden as affirmation that the Saudi government and clergy reject al-Qaeda's violence.[5]

1 Peter Baker, Helene Cooper & Mark Mazetti, "Bin Laden Is Dead, Obama Says," *The New York Times*, May 1, 2011, www.nytimes.com/2011/05/02/world/asia/osama-bin-laden-is-killed.html?_r=1&hp.

2 http://islamtoday.net/albasheer/artshow-12-149953.html.

3 Ibid.

4 Surendra Munshi, "Time To Heal the Wounds," *The Telegraph* (India), June 30, 2011, www.telegraphindia.com/1110630/jsp/opinion/story_14146877.jsp.

5 S. Iftikhar Murshed, "Al-Qaeda after Bin Laden," *The News International*, June 26, 2011, www.thenews.com.pk/TodaysPrintDetail.aspx?ID=54577&Cat=9; Munshi, "Time To Heal the Wounds;" Anissa Haddadi, "Al-Qaeda's 'Takfir' Killings Turn Muslims Away Before and After Death of Osama Bin Laden," *International Business Times*, June 9, 2011, www.ibtimes.com/articles/160261/20110609/al-qaeda-s-takfir-killings-turn-muslims-away-before-and-after-death-of-osama-bin-laden-ayman-al-zawa.htm.

Battling Online Extremism and the Call to Jihad

The Saudi battle against online extremism is a recent one. After September 11, many governments and media outlets condemned the kingdom for spreading extremist messages, as clerics continued to launch verbal attacks against Israel and call for *jihad* against American and allied forces in Iraq and Afghanistan.[6]

However, since al-Qaeda staged attacks in 2003 and 2004, and threatened the stability of the state, the Saudi religious establishment has painstakingly refuted the ideology and actions of bin Laden and al-Qaeda. Primarily, it seeks to re-empower the ruling family as the only authority permitted to sanction *jihad*.

The efforts of the Saudi government and its clerics to condemn those who commit "unauthorized" *jihad* were evident. In January 2011, Minister of Islamic Affairs Salih Al al-Sheikh said that the kingdom hoped to increase the integrity and effectiveness of Islamic *da'wa* (outreach) websites in an effort to spread "moderate" Islam and reject "deviant" and "extremist" ideas.[7] Later that same month, the Ministry organized a symposium with researchers and specialists to study and evaluate the effectiveness of internet advocacy in fighting terrorism and extremism.[8]

Weeks later, the Council of Senior Ulema and Grand Mufti Abdulaziz Al al-Sheikh vehemently denied issuing a *fatwa* in support of bin Laden, saying that the *fatwa* released under its name was fabricated. Al al-Sheikh said that, "What has been mentioned in the *fatwa* is a total lie as it goes against the previous statements... [Al-Qaeda's] words and actions have caused destruction for Islam and Muslims. Every sane person can easily understand that they are following a deviant path and that no Muslim should join al-Qaeda or approve its activities..."[9]

During a debate on the *al-Jazeera Talk* discussion forum, one user cited a *fatwa* from deceased cleric Muhammad ibn al-Othaimeen challenging the legality of suicide bombings. Al-Othaimeen ruled, "Whoever puts explosives on his body in order to put himself amongst a community of enemies, has killed himself, and

6 For examples, see: Nicolas Pelham, "Saudi Clerics Issue Edicts against Helping Infidels," *Christian Science Monitor*, October 12, 2001, www.csmonitor.com/2001/1012/p7s1-wome.html; "The House of Saud: The Fatwa of the 26 Clerics: Open Sermon to the Militant Iraqi People," *PBS Frontline*, February 8, 2005, www.pbs.org/wgbh/pages/frontline/shows/saud/etc/fatwa.html; Thomas Hegghammer, "Saudis in Iraq: Patterns of Radicalization and Recruitment," *Revues.org*, June 12, 2008, http://conflits.revues.org/index10042.html. In an "Open Sermon to the Militant Iraqi People," issued on November 5, 2004, on the eve of the American siege of Fallujah, twenty-six clerics signed on to a statement that legitimized participation in the Iraqi insurgency as part of a "defense jihad" against the "aggressor" coalition. The number of Saudis who went to Iraq to fight against Western forces is believed to have peaked after the sermon was released.

7 http://ksa.daralhayat.com/ksaarticle/225479.

8 www.alriyadh.com/2011/01/26/article598258.html.

9 Muhammad al-Sulaimi, "Dar Al-Ifta Denies Backing Al-Qaeda," *Arab News*, February 17, 2011, http://arabnews.com/saudiarabia/article266898.ece.

would be tortured with the instruments he used for suicide in eternal fire..."[10]

Saleh al-Fawzan also generated significant attention in January 2011, when he called the suicide bombers who attacked the Coptic Church in Alexandria, Egypt followers of Satan, and asserted that Muslims are prohibited from killing themselves.[11]

But many clerics appeared more concerned with distinguishing who may "legally" declare *jihad*, and reminding Muslims that they may only heed their ruler's call to religious violence.

On his personal website, the Grand Mufti explicitly rules out *jihad* for individuals, even when "apostates" enter Islamic lands. "Individual citizens should not get involved with security matters...It is up the rulers of the land to assess the intentions of non-Muslims and decide what course of action to take towards them."[12]

The Permanent Committee for Research and Ifta advised one individual that, "*Jihad*...becomes obligatory when the Muslim ruler declares a general struggle and commands you to go to war or when the person is actually involved in the battle. In such cases...no one is allowed to give priority to people over Allah's command."[13]

This was a trend that ConStrat even identified among bloggers. For example, the blog *Nuha38317.blogspot* cited *fatawa*—mostly from Saudi clerics—critical of violent, unauthorized *jihad*. The blog prominently featured videos that condemned al-Qaeda ideologue Anwar al-Awlaki (killed by the United States in late September 2011), and highlighted *tafseer* from cleric Abdul Muhsin al-Ubeikan describing jihadists as selfish.[14]

Websites That Spread "Extremism"

In October, Dr. Abdul Rahman al-Hadlaq, director-general of the Department of Intellectual Security for the Saudi Ministry of Interior, reported that 6,000 websites around the world still spread "extremism." Interestingly, the Saudis are careful not to grant the title of "jihadist" to online activists who engage in extremism. According to al-Hadlaq, "we do not need to classify those owners of deviant thought 'jihadists' because they rejoice in this title...the correct name for them is the 'deviant group'."[15]

10 http://aljazeeratalk.net/forum/showthread.php?t=327166&page=4. (Thread no longer available; Accessed via VX on April 2, 2011)

11 "Saudi Cleric Sees Devil behind Suicide Attacks," *The Daily Star*, January 8, 2011, www.dailystar.com.lb/News/Middle-East/Jan/08/Saudi-cleric-sees-devil-behind-suicide-attacks.ashx#axzz1WihSlApX.

12 For the website of Grand Mufti Abdulaziz Al al-Sheikh, see www.mufti.af.org.sa.

13 For the complete *fatwa*, see http://en.islamtoday.net/node/1218.

14 http://nuha38317.blogspot.com/search/label/Jihad%20and%20the%20Martyr.

15 http://ksa.daralhayat.com/ksaarticle/315818.

While ConStrat did not identify 6,000 radical sites during the collection period, it identified a number of them published in English and Arabic that forwarded intolerant or radical discourse in connection with Saudi clerics.

In English:
Ummah (http://ummah.com) hosted discussions on various Muslim issues, such as the establishment of the Palestinian state and fundraising for Afghan refugees. Most of the radical content was related to discussions about the concept of *jihad* and legitimate Islamic governance.[16]

Siratemustaqeem (http://siratemustaqeem.com) discussed religious beliefs in Islam and *fatawa* related to *shirk* (apostasy) in the Islamic faith. Conversations about "true" forms of monotheism usually led to discussions on *takfeer* (excommunication), which generated radical commentary.[17]

In Arabic:
Muslm.net (www.muslm.net) is a popular site that hosted highly intense religious and political debates on historic and contemporary issues. The web-users who frequented this site tended to be sympathetic to Wahhabi ideology and supportive of jihadist movements.[18]

Paldf (www.paldf.net), the Palestine Dialogue Forum, focused on news regarding Palestinian issues, but included an "Islamic resistance" narrative and a *Shari'ah* forum. Discussants often referenced Saudi clerics; some people disparaged ibn Baz's rejection of suicide attacks, claiming that Saudi *fatawa* are not universal and do not apply to the Palestinian case.[19]

Noor el-Islam (www.noor-elislam.net) was a self-described Salafi forum that attempted to explain the *Quran* and *Ahadith* (sayings of the Prophet Muhammad) based on the "true teaching of the Prophet Muhammad and his followers." Users supported a *fatwa* from ibn Baz that promotes social and religious intolerance. In one thread, they cited ibn Baz's warning against "traveling to the land of infidels," because of "its negative effects on creed and morality."[20] Others circulated several radical *fatawa* by Rabia al-Madkhali, who opposes women driving and argues that anyone who believes in freedom of religion is an apostate.[21]

16 "Jihad or Khalifah, Which Comes First," www.ummah.com/forum/showthread.php?282608-Jihad-or-Khilafah-which-comes-1st.

17 Accessed via VX.

18 www.muslm.net.

19 www.paldf.net/forum/showthread.php?t=824791&page=6.

20 http://noor-elislam.net/vb/showthread.php?t=13796.

21 http://noor-elislam.net/vb/showthread.php?t=13855.

Almoslim (www.almoslim.net), which is administered by *Sahwa* cleric Nasir al-Omar, openly denigrated Shi'a Muslims and expressed enmity toward the West. *Fatawa* on this site were often hostile to reforms, such as Grand Mufti Abdulaziz Al al-Sheikh's ruling that "proponents of women's emancipation are advocates of evil and misguidance."[22]

Clerics for Jihad

While Saudi clerics now explicitly oppose—or at least provide caveats against—al-Qaeda's religious justifications and tactics, current and former clerics' *fatawa* still provide ammunition to jihadists.

Hamud ibn Uqla al-Shuaibi, who died in 2001, was a proponent of suicide attacks and celebrated by al-Qaeda in the Arabian Peninsula (AQAP). Based on the sample that ConStrat culled, his *fatawa* live on in the hearts of Saudi extremists.

Molded from the core of the Wahhabi system, al-Shuaibi studied under former Grand Muftis Muhammad ibn Ibrahim Al al-Sheikh and ibn Baz, and then taught several high-profile members of the Saudi establishment, including the current Grand Mufti and Salman al-Odah. Al-Shuaibi's personal website offers his *fatwa* on suicide bombings, which concludes: "Martyrdom operations...are legitimate in religion, a *jihad* for Allah, if the intention of the perpetrator is pure. They are one of the most successful means of *jihad* and effective means against the enemies of this religion...its legitimacy is proven by evidence from the *Quran* and *Sunnah* and scholarly consensus..."[23]

But support for *jihad* did not come only from deceased clerics. Muhammad al-Munajjid's *Islam Q&A* website (available as an iTunes app) also provides religious justifications for violence. In one entry, Al-Munajjid says, "[The Caliph]...must strive in *jihad* against those who stubbornly reject Islam after being called to it, until they become Muslim or agree to live under Muslim protection and pay *jizyah* (tax on non-Muslims), so...[Allah's] religion will prevail over all others."[24]

Even Salman al-Odah, who is frequently labeled a moderate, supported *jihad*. "*Jihad* means fighting the infidels and the like—this is the duty of the people of the country that has been dominated or occupied by the infidels. The rest of the Muslims must assist and support them."[25] He published this opinion in 2010, but it is still available on his *Islam Today* website.

22 http://almoslim.net/node/139995.

23 For al-Shuaibi's ruling on "martyrdom operations," see his website, www.al-oglaa.com/?section=subject&SubjectID=169.

24 www.islam-qa.com/en/ref/21509.

25 www.islamtoday.net/salman/artshow-28-138541.htm.

Enduring Saudi Radicalism toward Israel

In October 2011, one week after Israel and Hamas completed a prisoner swap—Israeli soldier Gilad Shalit in exchange for more than 1,000 Palestinian prisoners—Saudi cleric Awad al-Qarnee offered a $100,000 reward to any Palestinian who could kidnap an Israeli soldier for bargaining leverage in future prisoner deals. The cleric wrote on his Facebook page, "The press reported that the Zionist settlers will pay huge amounts of money to [whoever] kills the freed Palestinian prisoners... In response to these criminals I declare to the world that any Palestinian who will jail an Israeli soldier and exchange him for prisoners will be rewarded with a $100,000 prize."[26]

Then, billionaire Prince Alwaleed bin Talal's brother Khaled increased the reward offered by al-Qarnee to $1 million. He said, "I tell Dr. Awad, I will be in solidarity with you and pay the remaining $900,000 to take an Israeli soldier prisoner so that other prisoners can be freed."[27]

Finally, Awad's cousin and fellow cleric Aidh al-Qarnee also joined the chorus. Aidh told the London-based daily *al-Hayat*, "I ask Allah for martyrdom in his path, for the conquest of Jerusalem, and if *jihad* in the path of Allah is undertaken, I ask Allah to be one of his faithful soldiers." He further expressed his thanks "to all who struggle with their tongue, their money, their blood, or their knowledge, [against] the Zionist entity."[28]

Thus, while the Saudi clerics almost universally condemn al-Qaeda and what they define as "terrorism," they still support "legitimate" *jihad*. This only serves to reinforce long-held perceptions about the dangers of Wahhabism, and skepticism that the Saudi government is serious about eradicating the religious justifications that give rise to violence. To convince the global community that they are serious about fighting extremism, the Saudis will ultimately need to tackle this problem.

26 Roee Nahmias, "Saudi Cleric: Kidnap Soldier – Get $100,000," *Ynet News*, October 25, 2011, www.ynetnews.com/articles/0,7340,L-4138982,00.html.

27 "Saudi Prince Backs Cleric's Bounty Offer for Israeli Soldier," Reuters, October 29, 2011, www.reuters.com/article/2011/10/29/us-saudi-israel-bounty-idUSTRE79S32220111029.

28 http://ksa.daralhayat.com/ksaarticle/324903.

Conclusion

With protests still raging around the Arab world, new challenges may await the Saudi state. The protests may, in turn, also create new challenges for the West.

When FDD commissioned this study in late 2010, such political turmoil appeared highly unlikely, if not impossible. Our hope was to understand, nearly a decade after the 9/11 attacks, how Saudi clerics use the online space, including social media, to disseminate their messages, and the extent to which Saudi Arabia is involved in tempering or exacerbating the problem of online radicalization.

Our findings, largely gleaned from ConStrat's data, include the following:

The amount of overtly violent messages is marginal and declining: Militant entries that explicitly endorsed or condoned violence accounted for a small fraction of the postings scored. We believe this is because the Saudi government closely monitors and censors the internet as part of its battle against "deviants." Interestingly, the English language sites were more likely to address militant issues than Arabic ones, though some radical messaging remained.

Highly conservative, intolerant, and xenophobic content remains substantial: Such content accounted for between half and three-quarters of the postings that ConStrat scored.[1] In other words, while sanctioned and unsanctioned clerics have cut back on overtly violent rhetoric, they still view Western culture with disdain, exhibit a lack of respect for women's rights, and speak with open hostility about minorities, other religions, and non-Wahhabi Muslims.

Arab protest movements have opened up political debate for Saudi clerics: After an initial period of reticence, the clerics began to weigh in on the injustices of other regional governments and even Saudi allies, but largely spared the Saudi state. Their vocal response is a significant development, especially in light of the crackdown on the *Sahwa* clerics (and their eventual co-opting) in the early 1990s. Clerics may yet play a role in opening up political discourse in Saudi society.

1 See appendices for VX Ecosystem graphics.

New media and technology are becoming the clerics' preferred outlets: In addition to social media outlets like Twitter, Facebook, and YouTube, apps for iPhone, iPod, and iPad are gaining popularity among Saudi clerics. This phenomenon contradicts the religious establishment's historical opposition to "corrupting" modern technology.

Only a handful of clerics account for most of the traffic: Two sanctioned clerics—Saleh al-Fawzan and former Grand Mufti Abdulaziz ibn Baz—and one unsanctioned cleric—Salman al-Odah—accounted for the bulk of Arabic traffic. In English, al-Fawzan and al-Odah also ranked in the top three. Safar al-Hawali, who is unsanctioned, was the only other cleric who ranked in the top five for both languages.

Official clerics still "rubber stamp" regime policies: The state-sponsored clergy do not challenge the regime in any significant way, and often issue rulings that serve to buttress the regime against opposition, perceived or actual. While many users looked to the sanctioned clerics for rulings on daily Muslim life, some mocked them for serving as agents of the monarchy.

Clerics self-police: Unsanctioned clerics continue to expand their presence online, but rarely challenge the regime directly. More often than not, they provide additional support to the sanctioned clerics. This may date back to the co-opting of the *Sahwa* clerics. It may also be a result of the Saudi state's restrictive internet policies, which have likely forced the clerics to self-police.

While this study was primarily designed to help inform our understanding of the Saudi online environment, we can issue two broad policy recommendations:

Encourage the Saudi government to accelerate reforms: Among FDD's findings, the most important is that the Saudi government's efforts to restrict militant online content from its religious establishment have been effective. ConStrat identified only marginal numbers of overtly violent messages related to the Saudi clerics. This is a sign that the Saudis can, when sufficiently motivated, temper the radicalism that has long percolated in the kingdom. It is also a sign that U.S. pressure, when applied properly, can have a noticeable impact.

However, the kingdom's recent attempts to convince the West that it is promoting "religious tolerance"[2] and embracing change[3] do not resonate with the online content mined for this study. *Jihad*-related content aside, ConStrat found that Saudi Arabia's religious establishment still openly denigrates other religions and cultures, and fails to adapt to modern social and scientific concepts.

2 "Saudi-Backed Religious Tolerance Center Opens in Vienna," *Al-Arabiya*, October 13, 2011, www.alarabiya.net/articles/2011/10/13/171684.html.

3 "A Promise of Reform in Saudi Arabia," *The New York Times*, February 5, 2009, www.nytimes.com/2009/02/26/opinion/26thu2.html.

Recent examinations of official high school textbooks further confirm the online data. Though the government repeatedly pledges to remove "intolerant" content from the country's textbooks, passages remain that speak about fighting the Jews to bring about the hour of judgment, describe women as weak and irresponsible, and call for homosexuals to be put to death because they pose a danger to society.[4] This is troubling, considering that Saudi Arabia is described as one of America's most important Middle East allies. This stark lack of shared values has encumbered the relationship in the past, and raises questions about the future.

Monitor online activity of the clerics and their followers: The Saudi social media environment requires further assessment, and is deserving of ongoing observation by the intelligence community (for threats) and State Department (for diplomacy and de-radicalization opportunities). We have long held that, coupled with other reporting streams, online research can greatly enhance our understanding of complex policy problems. In the case of Saudi Arabia, where the government limits access to the country, thorough online research can be particularly valuable.

If gathered properly, online sentiment can provide intelligence and insights in other important areas. The Saudis' ongoing challenges in fighting terrorism finance, education reform, and political change are obvious areas that could benefit from deeper online research.

A Final Word of Warning

The Saudi clerics are gaining influence through the use of online communication tools. New media are allowing them to communicate with the Saudi public and wider Muslim world on an unprecedented scale. Since they have generally not stepped over the Saudi government's "red lines," they have typically been unhindered.

To be sure, the relatively free flow of information in Saudi Arabia should be welcomed. But there may be a downside. As the unsanctioned clerics increasingly turn to various online platforms like Twitter, Facebook, and YouTube—and less to traditional state-controlled media outlets—the Saudi regime may find it more difficult to control their messages. The spike in clerical activity online translates directly to increased leverage and power.

Eventually, emboldened clerics may pose a direct challenge to the regime. During the 20th century alone, Saudi Arabia had three major confrontations with elements of the religious establishment: during the 1920s, when the zealous *Ikhwan*

4 Leon Watson, "The Arabic School Textbooks Which Show Children How To Chop Off Hands and Feet Under Sharia Law," *The Daily Mail*, December 23, 2011, www.dailymail.co.uk/news/article-2077658/The-Arabic-textbooks-children-chop-hands-feet-Sharia-law.html.

rebelled against ibn Saud; in 1979, when the Salafi separatist group *al-Jama'a al-Salafiyya al-Muhtasiba* held the Grand Mosque in Mecca hostage; and in the early 1990s, as the *Sahwa* clerics denounced the Western military presence in the Gulf and demanded a more Islamic Saudi government and society.

In all of those situations, the government successfully quelled dissent with a mix of draconian measures and co-opting strategies. But Saudi Arabia, like the rest of the Arab world, is now dealing with a new and rapidly changing political environment that looks nothing like the past.

Appendix 1: Cleric Index

Yusuf al-Ahmed: Unsanctioned; professor at Muhammad ibn Saud Islamic University in Riyadh; arrested in July 2011 after posting YouTube videos that criticized the indefinite detention of prisoners in Saudi Arabia; criticized the government-supported policy of allowing women to work as supermarket cashiers; described King Abdullah University for Science and Technology, the Kingdom's only co-educational facility, as part of a "Westernizing" project.[1]

Muhammad al-Arefe: Unsanctioned; preacher at al-Bawardi Mosque in Riyadh and faculty member at King Saud University;[2] more than 1,044,000 Twitter followers and 855,000 "likes" of his Facebook page as of March 2012;[3] heavily criticized for his remarks about women, especially a YouTube video in which he explains methods for a man to discipline his wife;[4] often issues inflammatory sermons that slander Shi'a Muslims.[5]

Abdul Rahman al-Barrak: Unsanctioned; denounced protests in Yemen as *haram* (forbidden), and a *fitna* (discord) which must be avoided;[6] reversed course regarding protests in Egypt, describing them as a "testament to God's power;"[7] condemned the driving campaign launched by Saudi women, calling them "women who open the gates of evil, seeking to westernize the country."[8]

Abdulaziz ibn Baz (d. 1999): Sanctioned; former Grand Mufti and former chairman of Muslim World League's Constituent Council; influential in online social media; emphasized the responsibility of Islamic states and organizations

1 "Saudi Arabia: Free Islamic Scholar Who Criticized Ministry," Human Rights Watch, July 14, 2011, www.hrw.org/news/2011/07/14/saudi-arabia-free-islamic-scholar-who-criticized-ministry.

2 See Muhammad al-Arefe's curriculum vitae on his personal website, http://arefe.com/PCV.aspx.

3 For Muhammad al-Arefe's Twitter page, see http://twitter.com/MohamadAlarefe; For his Facebook page, see www.facebook.com/3refe.

4 www.youtube.com/watch?v=PJGjC1rsQXs&feature=player_embedded#!.

5 "Saudi Cleric Muhammad Al-Arifi Exposes Shiites and Their History-Affairs," YouTube, November 7, 2010, www.youtube.com/watch?v=3651za7DBN0&feature=related.

6 http://almoslim.net/node/143433.

7 www.ajurry.com/vb/showthread.php?s=e0a50e83a3fa8b4edbbf31f95d04fbc8&p=56227#post56227.

8 http://alanba.com.kw/AbsoluteNMNEW/templates/last2010.aspx?articleid=198634&zoneid=29.

to support *mujahideen* (Islamic fighters) throughout the world;[9] issued a *fatwa* in 1991 banning women from driving.[10]

Saad al-Buraik: Unsanctioned; called for "smashing the skulls of those who organize demonstrations or take part in them;" has been described as "an extremist but also a government loyalist... in state-funded institutions."[11]

Nasir al-Fahd: Unsanctioned; one of several radical Saudi clerics who supported al-Qaeda's attacks in the kingdom; arrested in fall 2003 and subsequently renounced his support for militancy on Saudi television;[12] well known for a 2003 *fatwa* arguing that WMDs are permissible for use in *jihad* if there is no other way to defeat one's enemies.[13]

Saleh al-Fawzan: Sanctioned; Council of Senior Ulema member; popular in online social media; condemned the January 2011 bombing of the Coptic church in Alexandria, Egypt, calling it the work of Satan;[14] gained notoriety for asserting that a Muslim should kill a co-worker who does not pray,[15] and that fathers may arrange marriages for their daughters "even if they are in the cradle."[16]

Ahmed al-Ghamdi: Sanctioned; formerly headed the Mecca branch of the Committee for the Promotion of Virtue and Prevention of Vice (religious police); social activists have praised him for his opposition to gender segregation, full-body veils (*niqab*), and the ban on women driving.[17]

Safar al-Hawali: Unsanctioned; popular in online social media; became synonymous with the *Sahwa* (awakening) movement that challenged the Saudi government's Islamic credentials during the early 1990s; has moderated his stance toward the Saudi regime, but continues to inspire hatred and violence against Israel.[18]

9 Gold, *Hatred's Kingdom*, p. 119.

10 Bronson, *Thicker Than Oil*, pp. 210-211.

11 Al-Rasheed, "Preachers of Hate as Loyal Subjects."

12 Jones, "The Clerics, the Sahwa and the Saudi State," p. 4.

13 Will McCants, "Nasir Al-Fahd's Ruling on WMD," *Jihadica*, June 5, 2008, www.jihadica.com/nasir-al-fahds-ruling-on-wmd/.

14 "Saudi Cleric Sees Devil behind Suicide Attacks," *The Daily Star*, January 8, 2011, www.dailystar.com.lb/News/Middle-East/Jan/08/Saudi-cleric-sees-devil-behind-suicide-attacks.ashx#axzz1WihSIApX.

15 www.alhilalclub.com/vb/showthread.php?t=268543.

16 McDowall & Said, "Cleric Fights Saudi Bid to Ban Child Marriages."

17 For a collection of articles on al-Ghamdi by Eman al-Nafjan, see: http://saudiwoman.wordpress.com/2010/04/25/the-man-of-the-hour/; http://saudiwoman.wordpress.com/2011/01/26/the-commision-for-the-promotion-of-virtue-and-prevention-of-vices/; http://saudiwoman.wordpress.com/2011/04/03/going-back-in-time/#comment-9062.

18 For Safar al-Hawali's personal website, see www.alhawali.com/en/index.cfm?method=home.con&ContentId=6467.

Abdullah ibn al-Jibreen (d. 2009): Sanctioned; former member of the Permanent Committee for Research and Ifta (issuing *fatawa*); one of his *fatawa* suggested that the Earth is flat and the sun revolves around it;[19] endorsed al-Qaeda's violent 2003 attacks in Saudi Arabia.[20]

Ahmed al-Khalidi: Unsanctioned; endorsed al-Qaeda's violent 2003 attacks in Saudi Arabia; arrested in fall 2003 and subsequently renounced his support for militancy on Saudi television.[21]

Ali al-Khudeir: Unsanctioned; endorsed al-Qaeda's violent 2003 attacks in Saudi Arabia, was arrested in fall 2003 and subsequently renounced his support for militancy on Saudi television.[22]

Saleh al-Luhaidan: Sanctioned; Council of Senior Ulema member; removed from his position as chief judge of Saudi Supreme Judicial Council after saying it was permissible to kill owners of satellite television channels that promote moral depravity;[23] issued a *fatwa* calling for *jihad* against the "atheist" Syrian government.[24]

Rabia al-Madkhali: Unsanctioned; professor at Muhammad ibn Saudi Islamic University in Medina; issued *fatawa* in opposition to women driving and argued that anyone who believes in freedom of religion is an apostate;[25] rejected protests as a means to achieve reform and branded revolutions a "Leninist-Stalinist evil."[26]

Muhammad al-Munajjid: Unsanctioned; popular on Twitter; administrator of website *Islam Question and Answer* (*Q&A*); described the Israeli-Palestinian conflict as an Islamic issue which will not be solved until "Muslims cooperate to find a solution, and wage an Islamic *jihad* against the Jews..."[27]

19 For his *fatwa*, see www.djelfa.info/vb/showthread.php?p=6360171.

20 Jones, "The Clerics, the Sahwa and the Saudi State."

21 Ibid.

22 Ibid.

23 "Major Reshuffle in Saudi Arabia," BBC News, February 14, 2009, http://news.bbc.co.uk/2/hi/middle_east/7890211.stm.

24 For excerpts of his call for *jihad*, see www.sarayanews.com/object-article/view/id/65679&reason=0.

25 http://noor-elislam.net/vb/showthread.php?t=13855.

26 http://forums.naseej.com/showthread.php?175845-%E5%E1-%C7%E1%CE%D1%E6%CC-%DD%ED-%C7%E1%E3%D9%C7%E5%D1%C7%CA-%E6-%C7%E1%DE%ED%C7%E3-%C8%C7%E1%CB%E6%D1%C7%CA-%E3%E4-%E3%E4%E5%CC-%C3%E5%E1-%C7%E1%D3%E4%C9-%E6-%C7%E1%CC%E3%C7%DA%C9%BF-%ED%CC%ED%C8-%C7%E1%DA%E1%C7%E3%C9-%C7%E1. (Thread no longer available; Accessed via VX on October 15, 2011)

27 For the complete *fatwa*, see www.islam-qa.com/en/ref/21977/solution%20to%20the%20palestinian%20issue.

Salman al-Odah: Unsanctioned; administrator of *Islam Today* website; popular on Twitter and other social media; gained prominence as one of the *Sahwa* clerics who criticized the Saudi government's Islamic credentials during the 1990-1991 Persian Gulf crisis; supported 2011 Arab protests and urged Turkish Prime Minister Erdogan to "not be a supporter to the criminals" in Syria.[28]

Nasir al-Omar: Unsanctioned; Secretary-General for Association of Muslim Scholars and administrator of *almoslim.net*; issued early *fatwa* against self-immolation; months later, called for the downfall of regimes in Yemen[29] and Syria[30]; openly denigrates Shi'a Muslims and expresses enmity toward the West.[31]

Muhammad ibn al-Othaimeen (d. 2001): Sanctioned; former Council of Senior Ulema Member; one *fatwa* ruled that a suicide bomber "would be tortured with the instruments he used for suicide in eternal fire..."[32]

Abdullah ibn al-Qaoud: Sanctioned; former member of Permanent Committee for Research and Ifta and Council of Senior Ulema; ruled that, "It is allowed for a woman to go see a male gynecologist if there are no female doctors available, but he [the doctor] shall not be with her [the patient] alone in the same room."[33]

Aidh al-Qarnee: Unsanctioned; weekly columnist for pan-Arab daily *Al-Sharq Al-Awsat*; popular on Twitter; claimed that it was *fitna* (discord) for Yemeni President Ali Abdullah Saleh to remain in power;[34] al-Qadhafi family reportedly requested his religious approval for the Libyan regime during the 2011 uprising;[35] supported women's right to drive in Saudi Arabia;[36] in one 2005 sermon, which supported Hamas' terrorism against Israel, he described Jews as the "brothers of apes and pigs and murderers of the prophets."[37]

28 http://islamtoday.net/albasheer/artshow-12-148590.htm.

29 www.almoslim.net/node/147641?sms_ss=twitter%26at_xt=4ded07c85870cb5f,0&reason=0.

30 http://almoslim.net/node/149506&reason=0.

31 See al-Omar's website, www.almoslim.net.

32 http://aljazeeratalk.net/forum/showthread.php?t=327166&page=4. (Thread no longer available; Accessed via VX on April 2, 2011)

33 http://alqaoud.net/word.php?t=2.

34 www.alarabiya.net/articles/2011/05/22/150092.html.

35 "Gaddafi's Sons Tried to Get Saudi Cleric Help," Reuters, February 28, 2011, http://af.reuters.com/article/libyaNews/idAFLDE71R1AT20110228.

36 http://islamtoday.net/albasheer/artshow-12-151273.htm; See also: www.alanba.com.kw/AbsoluteNMNEW/templates/last2010.aspx?articleid=200735&zoneid=29.

37 "Shaykh Aed Al Qarni – Jihad, the Path to Victory!" YouTube, September 5, 2009, www.youtube.com/watch?v=wrEEu-fjzqk.

Awad al-Qarnee: Unsanctioned; cousin of Aidh al-Qarnee; offered $100,000 to any Palestinian who could kidnap an Israeli soldier to be used in future prisoner swaps.[38]

Abdulaziz Al al-Sheikh: Sanctioned; current Grand Mufti; ruled that self-immolation is forbidden in Islam and a "heinous crime and a great calamity;"[39] declared that, "Proponents of women's emancipation" are "advocates of evil and misguidance;"[40] described Twitter as a site where people "issue [*fatawa*] without any knowledge... and to lie in a manner that brings fame to some."[41]

Muhammad ibn Ibrahim Al al-Sheikh (d. 1969): Sanctioned; former Grand Mufti; formerly chaired the Muslim World League's Constituent Council;[42] web-users cited him to bolster arguments for sex-segregated hospitals.[43]

Abdullah ibn Muhammad Al al-Sheikh: Sanctioned; son of former Grand Mufti Muhammad Al al-Sheikh and president of Saudi Shura (Consultation) Council.[44]

Hamud ibn Uqla al-Shuaibi (d. 2001): Unsanctioned; molded from the Wahhabi establishment's core; among the clerics who supported al-Qaeda's violence in Saudi Arabia in 2003 and 2004.[45]

Abdul Rahman al-Sudais: Sanctioned; *imam* of the Grand Mosque in Mecca; called for Muslims to peacefully co-exist and uphold moderate teachings,[46] but practiced *takfeer* against Sufis, and referred to Jews as "monkeys and pigs."[47]

Abdul Muhsin al-Ubeikan: Sanctioned; member of the Saudi Shura Council and advisor in the Royal Court; ruled that joining al-Qaeda is forbidden in Islam;[48] called jihadists selfish.[49]

38 Nahmias, "Saudi Cleric: Kidnap Soldier – Get $100,000."

39 http://ksa.daralhayat.com/ksaarticle/225894.

40 http://almoslim.net/node/139995.

41 "Saudi Grand Mufti: Twitter Is Full of Lies," *The Jerusalem Post*, January 28, 2012, www.jpost.com/MiddleEast/Article.aspx?id=255501.

42 Gold, *Hatred's Kingdom*, p. 119.

43 Sidiya & Al-Sulami, "Debate on Gender Mixing in Hospitals Moves from Facebook to Shoura."

44 www.aawsat.com/details.asp?section=68&article=661635&issueno=12119.

45 Jones, "The Clerics, the Sahwa and the Saudi State."

46 "Al-Sudais Speaks about Challenges Facing Islam," *Arab News*, April 21, 2011, http://arabnews.com/saudiarabia/article369488.ece.

47 Upadhyay, "Mecca Imam's Visit to India: Some Observations – Analysis."

48 Abdullah al-Oraifij, "Joining Qaeda is 'Haram': Al-Obeikan," *The Saudi Gazette*, January 12, 2010, www.saudigazette.com.sa/index.cfm?method=home.regcon&contentID=2010011259904.

49 http://nuha38317.blogspot.com/search/label/Jihad%20and%20the%20Martyr.

Appendix 2: ConStrat's Methodology

To explore the ideas the Saudi religious establishment promotes and how those ideas disseminate via the Internet, ConStrat conducted a six-month, two-phase study at the behest of FDD. From January 1, 2011 through June 30, 2011, ConStrat collected and coded data from thousands of Arabic and English language websites, forum threads, and social media posts, looking for *tafseer* or *fatawa* by Saudi clerics or social media commentary about them.

To maintain the linguistic and cultural nuances of the collected information, two ConStrat researchers with native Arabic language skills analyzed Arabic data, while two native English researchers with specialized academic and practical training in the Arabic language and Muslim culture analyzed English data. For comparative analysis between languages, researchers coded Arabic and English data separately.

In the first phase of the study, ConStrat analyzed hundreds of *tafseer* and *fatawa* on the personal websites of Saudi clerics and other websites where the clerics publish their commentary and opinions. The findings helped identify the topics clerics discussed most often, as well as their sentiments on those topics.

For the second phase of the study, ConStrat used two software platforms to mine the social media environment for mentions of Saudi clerics to explore how their messages are disseminated. ConStrat used its proprietary ***VX***® technology to collect and analyze data from online message boards (forums). From this analysis, ConStrat assessed the volume of forum discussions concerning Saudi clerics, the volume of forum discussions by topic, and discussion sentiments by topic. ***VX***® also identified forums in which Saudi clerics and *fatawa* were most discussed.

ConStrat also used the market research software ***ALTERIAN SM2***® to analyze mentions of Saudi clerics on additional social media platforms such as Twitter, Facebook, YouTube, and Blogger. The ***SM2***® analytical tool helped ConStrat researchers assess the volume of social media content related to Saudi clerics, the geographical reach of Saudi clerics' messages, and the top domains propagating commentary about the clerics.

ConStrat also measured how social media users engage with Saudi clerics online. Researchers measured engagement by looking at where Saudi clerics and social media users gravitated, which clerics and ideas were important to social media users, and where social media users consumed information about Saudi clerics.

ConStrat categorized clerics' *tafseer* and *fatawa*, as well as online users' commentary, into seven thematic topics, and then assigned a sentiment (See Methodology Chapter). Measuring sentiment was designed to characterize the tone of views that Saudi clerics expressed, as well as the tone of their followers' views. ConStrat researchers coded sentiment on a spectrum from moderate to militant; but it was merely an informal process designed to identify where certain topics, Internet domains, Saudi clerics, and social media users ranked on a relative spectrum. ConStrat fully acknowledges that sentiment analysis—particularly one that describes religious figures and ideas as radical or moderate—is a sensitive and widely debated subject.

It was also helpful to understand which social media users and venues were most influential. ConStrat researchers used ***SM2***®'s proprietary popularity measurement tool to identify the influence of social media users and venues propagating commentary on Saudi clerics. For each type of media, which included micro blogs, video and photo sharing sites, forums, blogs, and social networking sites, the software used separate metrics and algorithms to determine popularity.

Finally, ConStrat measured "reach" by indentifying the distribution of messages and commentary over different social networks, the number of "re-tweets" or comments on forums and blogs, as well as the linguistic and geographical distribution of the messages of Saudi clerics.

In conducting this study, ConStrat was fully cognizant of the fact that internet research does not paint the full picture of how the Saudi religious establishment propagates its ideology. These ideas are also widely distributed beyond the Internet, including via radio, television, print media and Saudi charities abroad. Moreover, even with experienced foreign media analysts from ConStrat using advanced analytical tools, the Internet is much too large for a single study to capture every mention of Saudi clerics. This was an earnest attempt to capture a snapshot of the Saudi clerical environment online, to be used as a springboard for discussion, as envisioned by FDD.

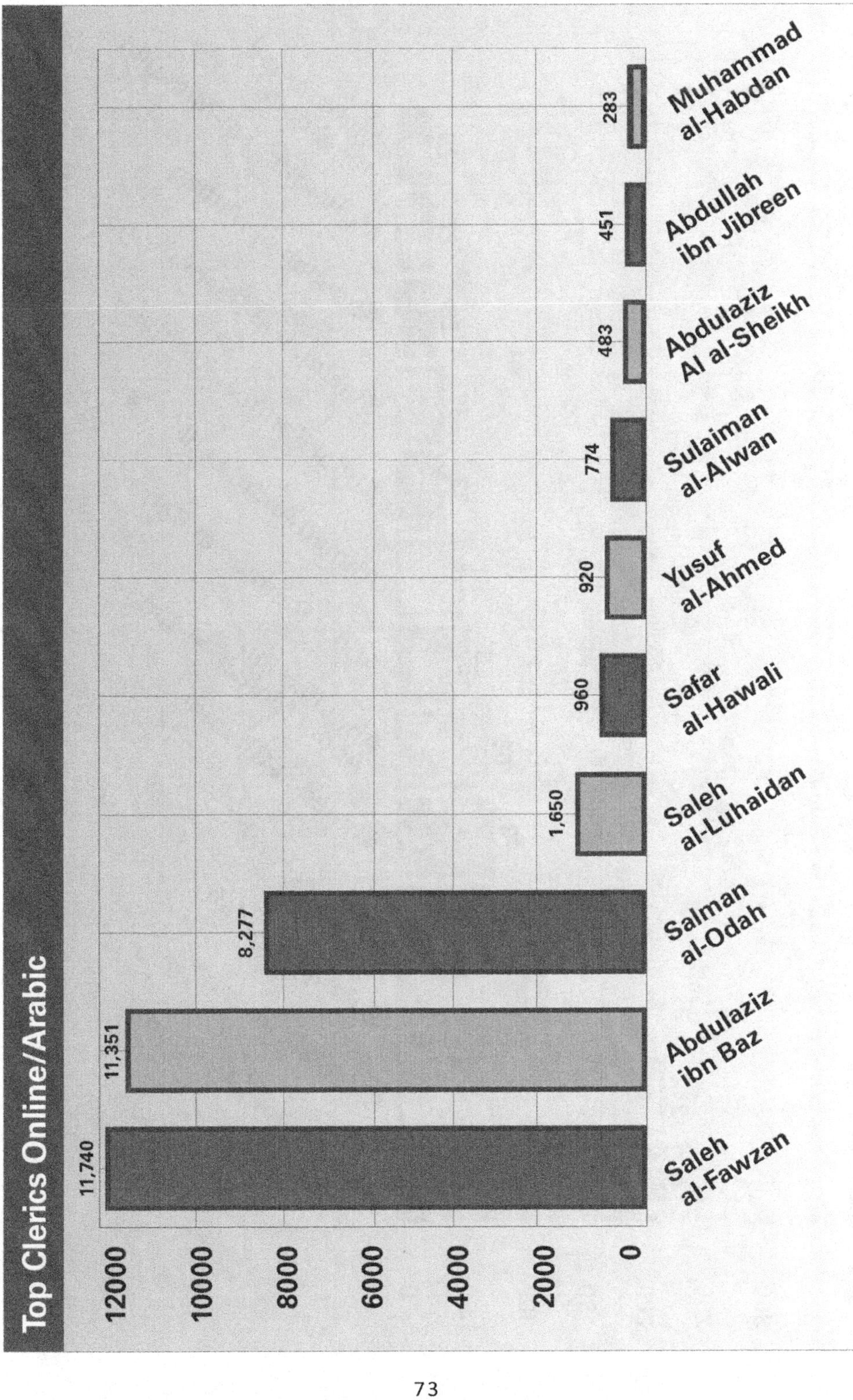
Top Clerics Online/Arabic
12000
10000
8000
6000
4000
2000
0
11,740
11,351
8,277
1,650
960
920
774
483
451
283
Saleh al-Fawzan
Abdulaziz ibn Baz
Salman al-Odah
Saleh al-Luhaidan
Safar al-Hawali
Yusuf al-Ahmed
Sulaiman al-Alwan
Abdulaziz Al al-Sheikh
Abdullah ibn Jibreen
Muhammad al-Habdan

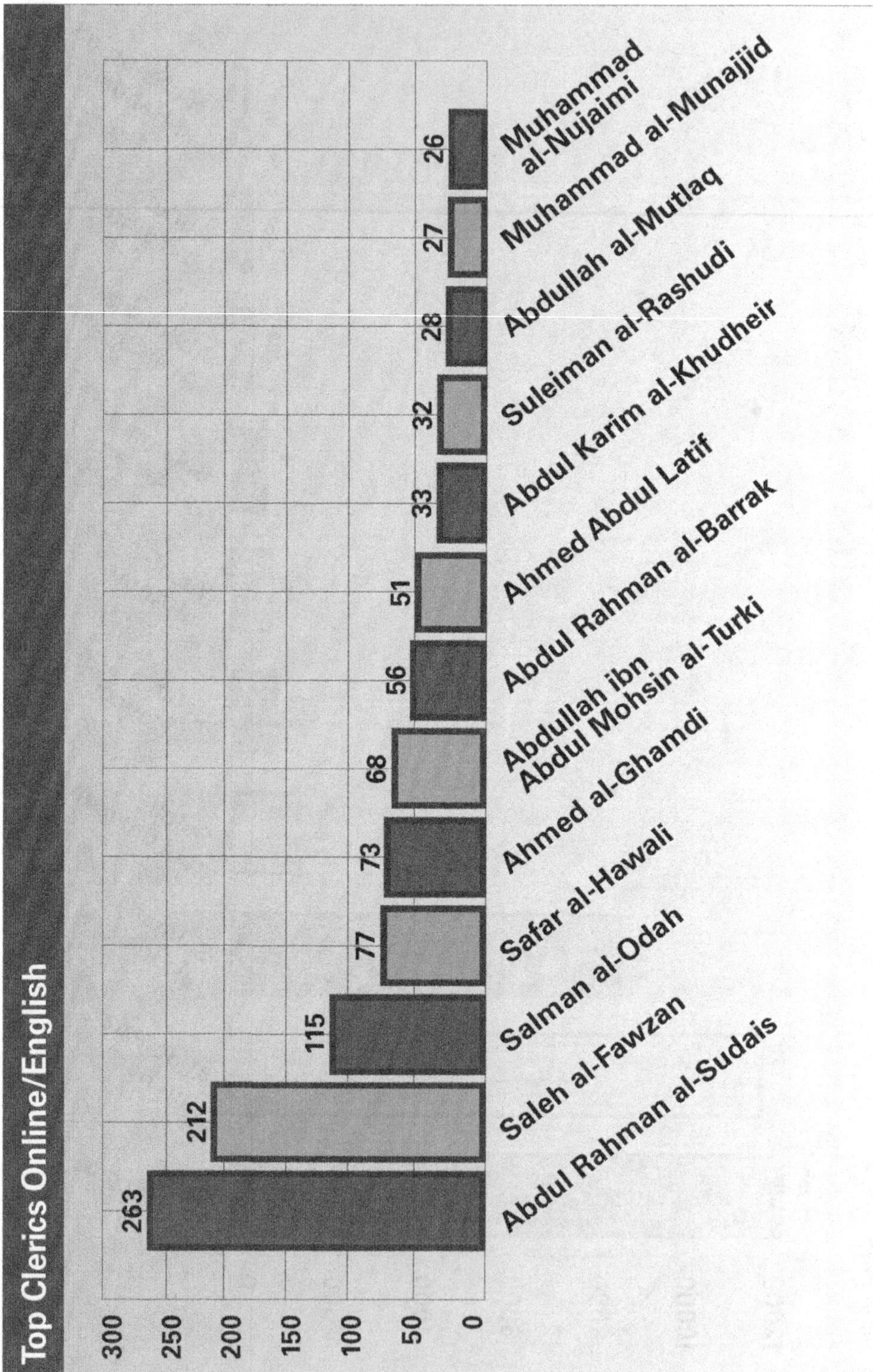
Top Clerics Online/English
300
250
200
150
100
50
0
263
212
115
77
73
68
56
51
33
32
28
27
26
Abdul Rahman al-Sudais
Saleh al-Fawzan
Salman al-Odah
Safar al-Hawali
Ahmed al-Ghamdi
Abdullah ibn Abdul Mohsin al-Turki
Abdul Rahman al-Barrak
Ahmed Abdul Latif
Abdul Karim al-Khudheir
Suleiman al-Rashudi
Abdullah al-Mutlaq
Muhammad al-Munajjid
Muhammad al-Nujaimi

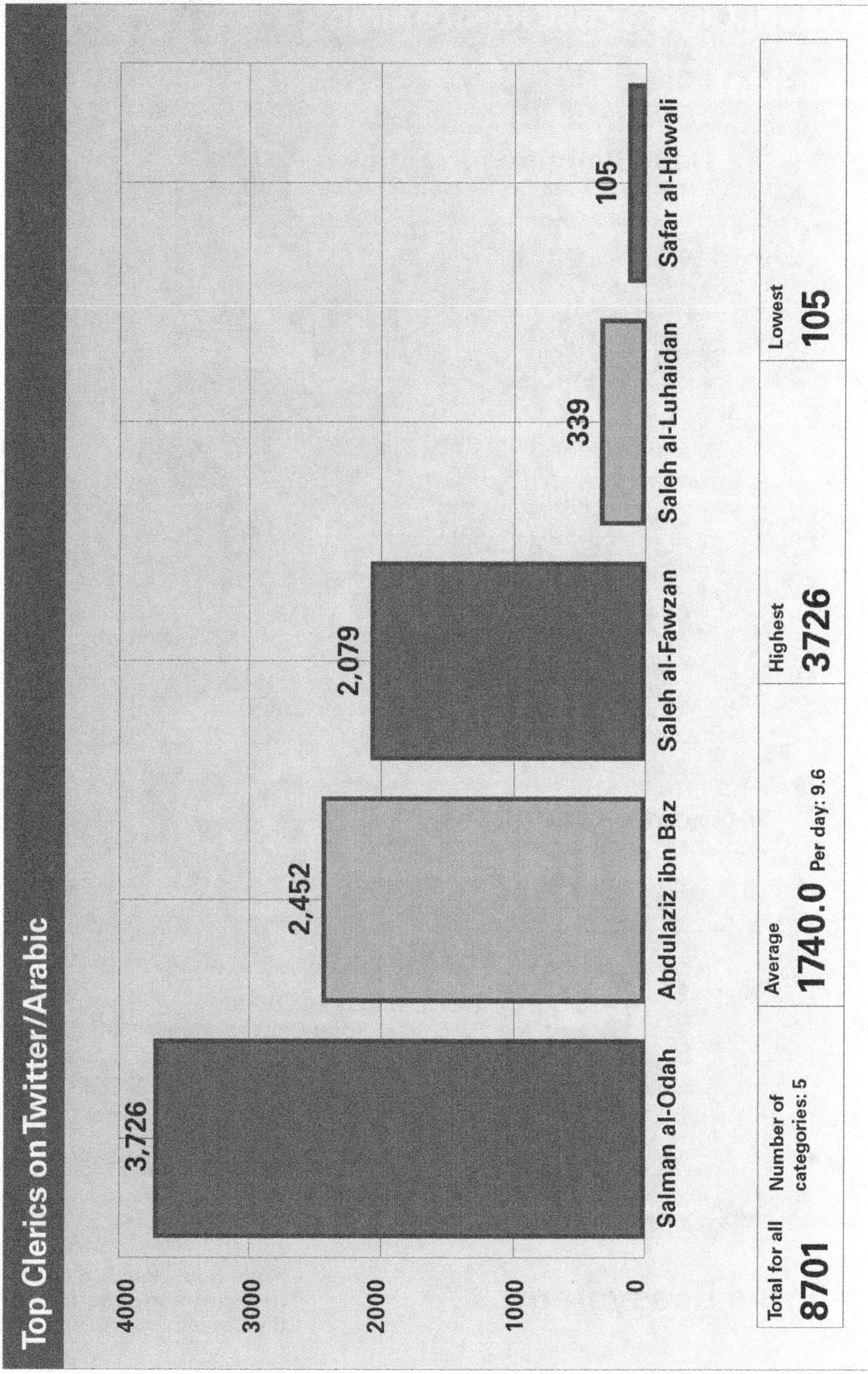
Top Clerics on Twitter/Arabic
4000
3000
2000
1000
0
3,726
2,452
2,079
339
105
Salman al-Odah
Abdulaziz ibn Baz
Saleh al-Fawzan
Saleh al-Luhaidan
Safar al-Hawali
Total for all
8701
Number of categories: 5
Average
1740.0
Per day: 9.6
Highest
3726
Lowest
105

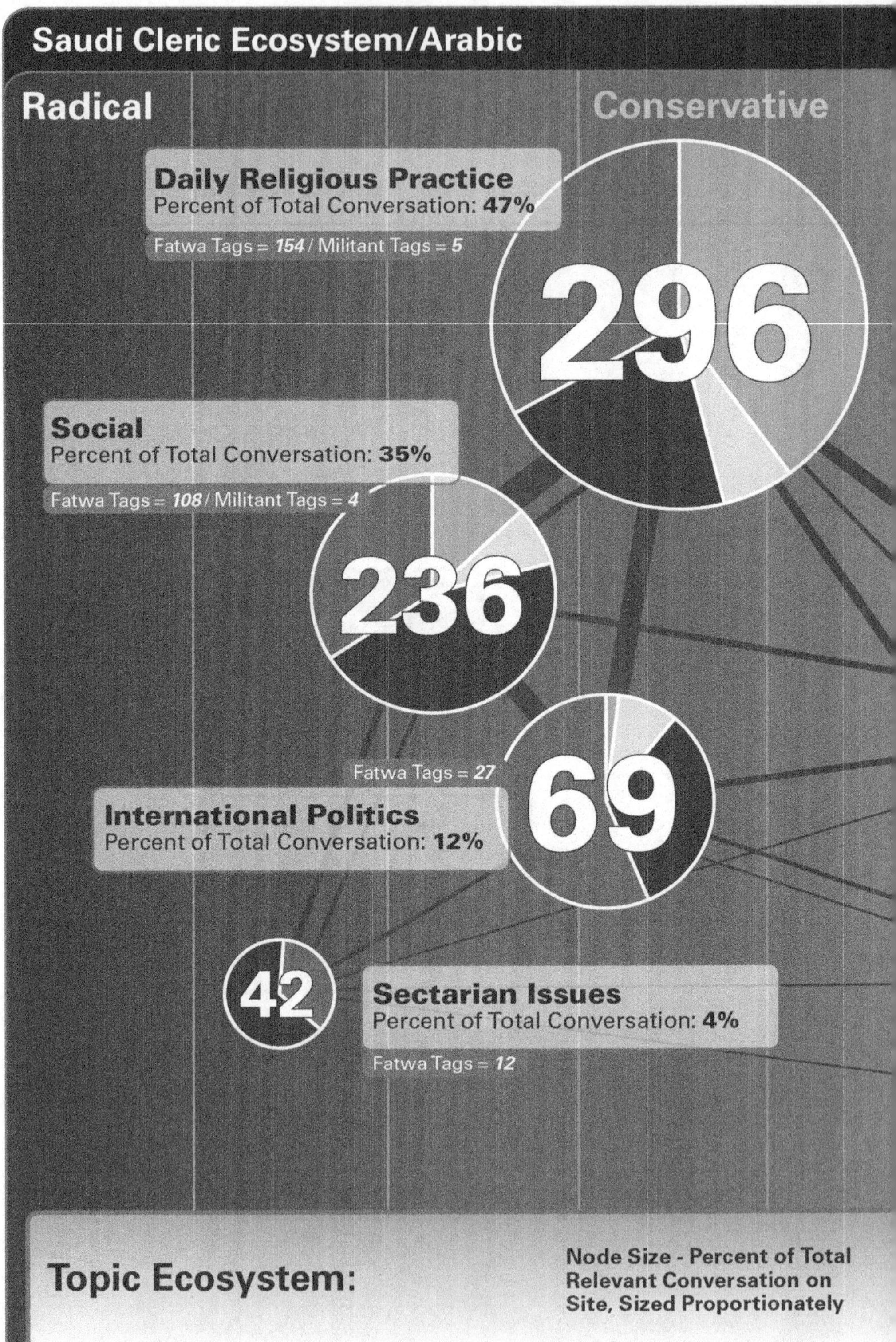
Saudi Cleric Ecosystem/Arabic
Radical
Conservative
Daily Religious Practice
Percent of Total Conversation: 47%
Fatwa Tags = 154 / Militant Tags = 5
296
Social
Percent of Total Conversation: 35%
Fatwa Tags = 108 / Militant Tags = 4
236
Fatwa Tags = 27
69
International Politics
Percent of Total Conversation: 12%
42
Sectarian Issues
Percent of Total Conversation: 4%
Fatwa Tags = 12
Topic Ecosystem:
Node Size - Percent of Total Relevant Conversation on Site, Sized Proportionately

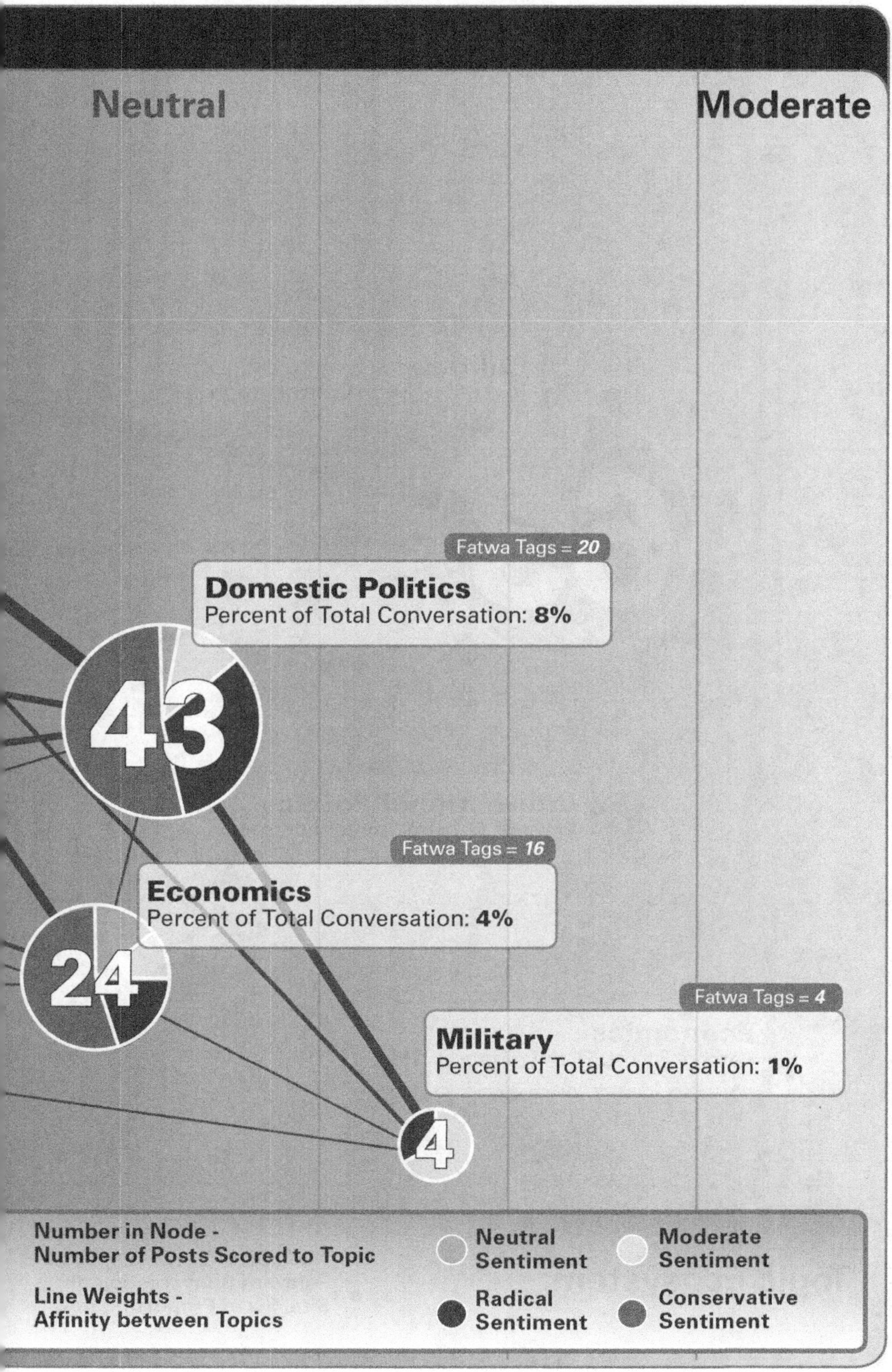
Neutral
Moderate
Fatwa Tags = 20
Domestic Politics
Percent of Total Conversation: 8%
43
Fatwa Tags = 16
Economics
Percent of Total Conversation: 4%
24
Fatwa Tags = 4
Military
Percent of Total Conversation: 1%
4
Number in Node - Number of Posts Scored to Topic
Line Weights - Affinity between Topics
Neutral Sentiment
Moderate Sentiment
Radical Sentiment
Conservative Sentiment

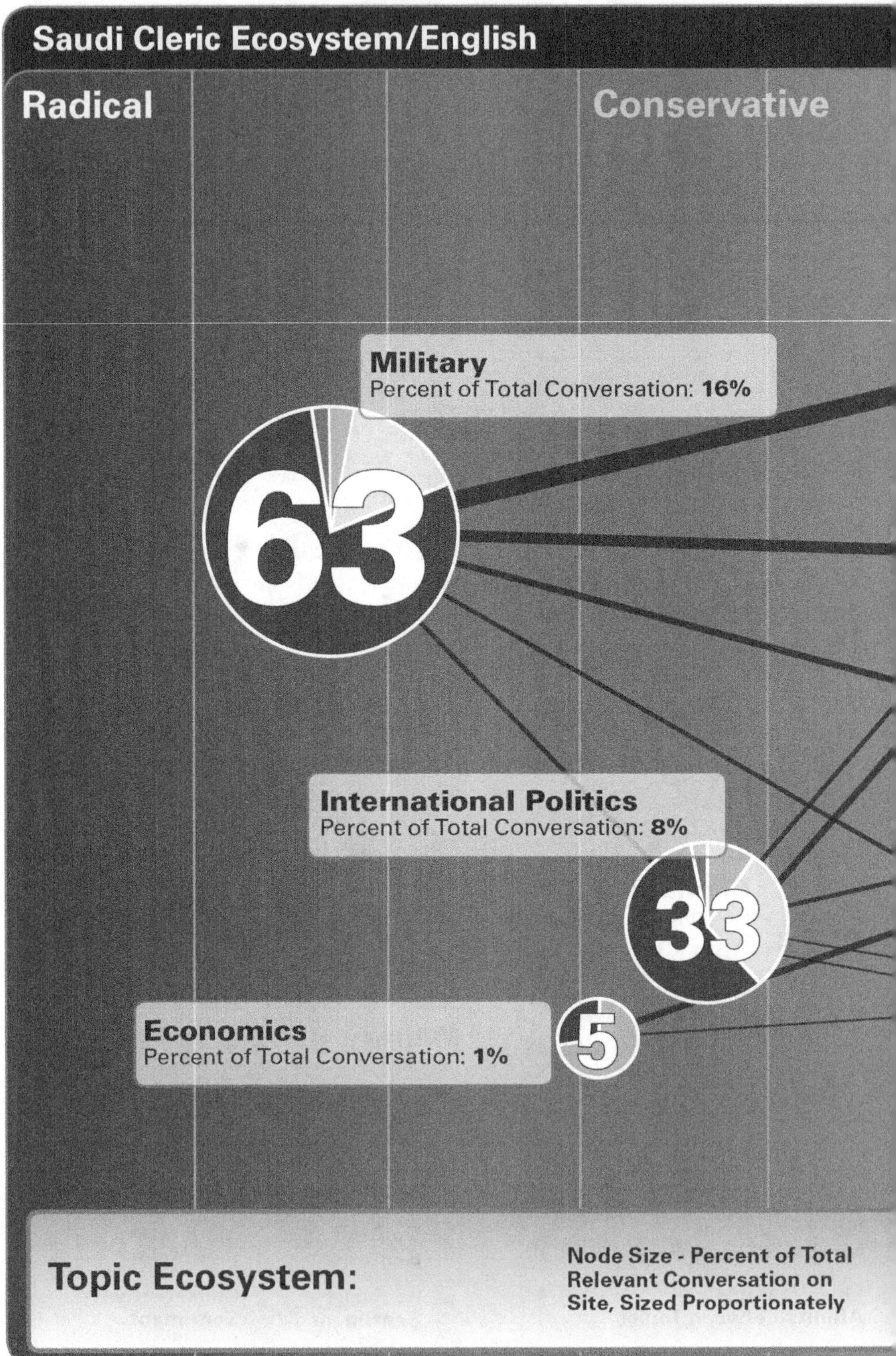
Saudi Cleric Ecosystem/English
Radical
Conservative
Military
Percent of Total Conversation: 16%
63
International Politics
Percent of Total Conversation: 8%
33
Economics
Percent of Total Conversation: 1%
5
Topic Ecosystem:
Node Size - Percent of Total Relevant Conversation on Site, Sized Proportionately

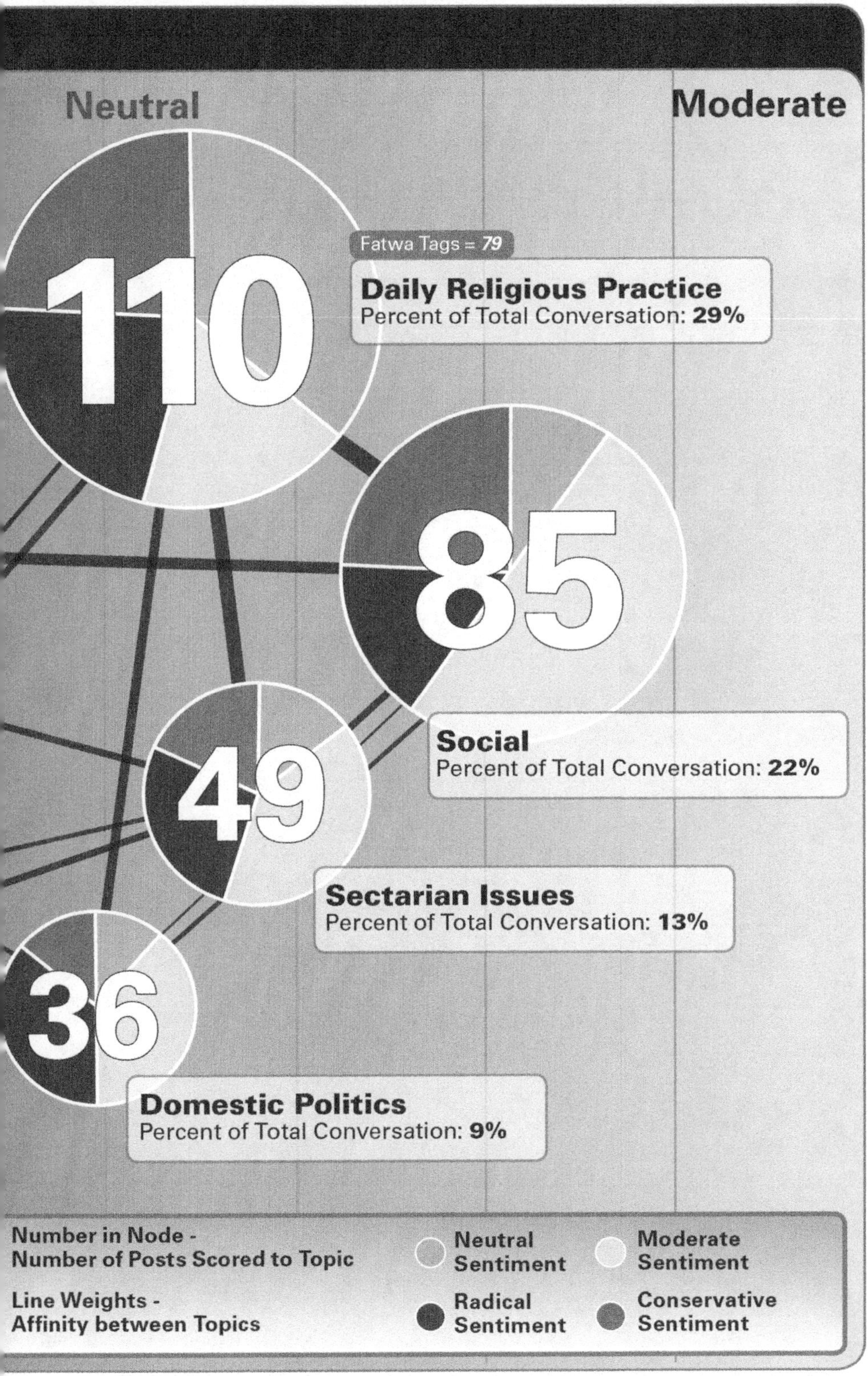
Neutral
Moderate
110
Fatwa Tags = 79
Daily Religious Practice
Percent of Total Conversation: 29%
85
Social
Percent of Total Conversation: 22%
49
Sectarian Issues
Percent of Total Conversation: 13%
36
Domestic Politics
Percent of Total Conversation: 9%
Number in Node -
Number of Posts Scored to Topic
Line Weights -
Affinity between Topics
Neutral Sentiment
Moderate Sentiment
Radical Sentiment
Conservative Sentiment

About the Authors

JONATHAN SCHANZER is Vice President for Research at the Foundation for Defense of Democracies. He is the author of *P@lestinian Pulse: What Policymakers Can Learn From Palestinian Social Media* (FDD Press, 2010), *Hamas vs. Fatah: The Struggle for Palestine* (Palgrave Macmillan, 2008) and *Al-Qaeda's Armies: Middle East Affiliate Groups and the Next Generation of Terror* (WINEP, 2004). Previously, he worked at the Washington Institute for Near East Policy and the Middle East Forum. From 2004 to 2007, Mr. Schanzer served as a counterterrorism analyst for the U.S. Department of the Treasury. He earned his PhD from King's College London.

STEVEN MILLER is a research associate at FDD, where he monitors and analyzes Arabic language press to help FDD scholars stay ahead of the curve on issues that are under-reported in the Western media. He also conducts research related to ideology and online media in Saudi Arabia, and his translations of Arabic language articles have been referenced in the media. Prior to joining FDD, Mr. Miller was a policy analyst at the Institute for Gulf Affairs, where he conducted research on Saudi Arabia's education curriculum and the security of Saudi Arabia's energy infrastructure. He studied Arabic at Indiana University.

Made in the USA
Monee, IL
13 September 2026

62981012R00059